FOUNDATIONS FOR SUCCESS

FOUNDATIONS FOR SUCCESS

52 Action Activities to Spark Your Personal Initiative

Napoleon Hill
&
Judith Williamson

PRABHAT PAPERBACKS

Published by
PRABHAT PAPERBACKS
4/19 Asaf Ali Road,
New Delhi-110 002 (INDIA)
e-mail: prabhatbooks@gmail.com

Published in India by arrangement with
The Napoleon Hill Foundation
PO Box 1277, Wise, Virginia 24293, USA

ISBN 978-93-5186-776-0
FOUNDATIONS FOR SUCCESS
by Napoleon Hill & Judith Williamson

Edition
2016

Price
₹ 200.00 (Rupees Two Hundred only)

Printed at
R-Tech Offset Printers, Delhi

Dedicated to all the readers of and contributors to the weekly "Napoleon Hill Yesterday and Today" e-zine.

Foreword

Dear Readers,

Foundations are essential for success in all walks of life. They provide the fundamental support that buildings, people, and organizations need in order to continue to grow. Without a firm footing at the beginning of any enterprise, few projects, people, or programs will succeed. Henry David Thoreau states:

> If you have built castles in the air, your work need not be lost; that is where they should be. Now put the foundations under them.

Once you read and also complete the exercises contained within the 52 chapters in this book, you will be primed to begin the pursuit of your own heart's desire. When this happens, you will no longer be standing on the sidelines watching things happen, but directly positioned on the inside making things happen.

Here is an example of how you might consider beginning to place *Foundations for Success* in your life right now.

Since Gourmet Coffee and Tea that makes people "Feel Good" is our business, imagine three equally sized coffee cups in front of you. If you consider your earnings, a good approach to balancing your life's finances would be to pour your income into the three cups. Let these cups represent your spending, your savings and your stewardship—that is, what you keep and use for yourself, what you save and use later for yourself and others, and what you give away right now for worthy programs.

Each time you receive income, divide the money into the three cups. Always allocate something for each. In this manner you will begin to realize that what you can do for yourself now, what you can do for you and your family later, and what you contribute to your community at large all play a very important role in establishing lifelong foundations that contribute to your enduring success.

Inside OrGano Gold, we make certain that our distributors are justly compensated for their sales, their families are provided for through our generational wealth programs, and the world community benefits too through the OG Cares Foundation. We take coffee cups seriously both in a literal and figurative manner. In doing so we create the foundational support that is essential to running a world class company because we care for our people, their families, and the world in which they live.

Once you begin at the personal level in seeing a bigger picture as to what your income can do, you will proceed to create a foundation for your own life that will not only serve you but others as well. When you begin now right where you are to look at the bigger picture, you will begin to grow and prosper in ever increasing ways.

Remember, it starts with a seed of thought, or in our case a coffee bean. We guarantee that when planted, nurtured and shared with good intention this seed will grow beyond your wildest imaginings. It all happens when you get the person—you—right. The rest of the process will fall into place almost upon command because a strong, permanent foundation has been laid.

Success is within you, and the process required to achieve it is a simple one. It begins with your realization that you are here to provide for yourself now, care for yourself and your family in the future, and simultaneously make the world a better place in which to live now because you have contributed in an ongoing way to its beautification program through your intentional stewardship.

May you believe and achieve all your heart's desires,

Shane & Josie Morand

CHAPTER 1

Lots of us have ideas—good ones, too—but no matter how good they may be, they are of little value unless we "follow through" on them.

– Jerome Waterman

This year's theme will be dedicated to making our world a better place in which to live—one week at a time. For 52 weeks, the "Napoleon Hill Yesterday and Today" columns will focus on simple things that each of us can do to make a positive contribution to the earth, our home. It's evident that in order to make something happen, we must first focus on it. Therefore, by bringing positive choices into focus, each of us can begin the New Year with a weekly target that will enhance our lives in small ways, but grow to impact the entire world as we all decide to contribute to the total "good choice" movement.

It only takes a moment for each of us to realize that something needs to be changed. By taking positive action toward that change, the moment of our personal dedication can become an empowered movement. Personal Moment to Global Movement! Many little actions soon add up to a lot. By letting little actions accumulate until they become too big to go unnoticed we begin to change the world. William James advises: "Act as if what you do makes a difference. It does."

Take a moment to reflect on the little things that changed your life for the better. Maybe it was a kind word, a short note, a pet your rescued, a person who lent a helping hand, a poem, a piece of art, a well-tended garden, holiday decorations, motivational quotes, or a small, personalized gift. Whatever it was, you rejoiced in the moment and then and there decided to go and do likewise. Now is your chance. Take up the challenge, and do something positive each week, daily, maybe hourly, to rescue this earth with one, heartfelt positive action at a time. Remember the starfish story? If you only save one, it makes a *huge* difference for that one!

Today, I will begin again to make a small contribution that indeed can change the world.

The Major Attributes of Personal Initiative

by Napoleon Hill

Personal initiative heads the list of qualities a successful leader must possess. These qualities are:

- Personal Initiative.
- The adoption of a definite major purpose.
- A motive to inspire continuous action in pursuit of a definite major purpose.
- A master mind alliance through which you may acquire the power to attain your definite purpose.
- Self-reliance in proportion to the scope and object of your major purpose.
- Self-discipline sufficient to insure mastery of the head and the heart, and to sustain your motives until they have been realized.
- Persistence, based on the will to win.
- A well-developed imagination, controlled and directed.
- The habit of reaching definite and prompt decisions.
- The habit of basing opinions on known facts instead of relying on guesswork.
- The habit of going the extra mile.
- The capacity to generate enthusiasm at will, and to control it.
- A well-developed sense of details.
- The capacity to take criticism without resentment.
- Familiarity with the ten basic motives that inspire all human action.

- The capacity to concentrate your full attention upon one task at a time.
- Willingness to accept full responsibility for the mistakes of subordinates.
- The habit or recognizing the merits and abilities of others.
- A positive mental attitude at all times.
- The habit of assuming full responsibility for any job or task undertaken.
- The capacity for applied faith.
- Patience with subordinates and associates.
- The habit of following through with any task once begun.
- The habit of emphasizing thoroughness instead of speed.

PMA Science of Success, Educational Edition. Napoleon Hill Foundation, 1961, pp. 201–202.

Action Assignment #1

Holiday Cards are so beautiful and yet difficult to recycle. Consider creating a postcard size mailer from the backside of each card and return the favor to the sender by writing a personalized note during the month of January. Just by taking a minute of your time and a few cents in postage, you can remind someone that they are special in your life and that you are thankful for the priceless gift of their friendship. This little gesture of remembering someone in a special way will be a unique way to say "thank you" and carry on the special cheer of the season.

Chapter 2

Don't just say "Happy New Year" or wish for a Happy New Year, but rather—make it a Happy New Year—one act at a time, one day at a time, for 52 consecutive weeks.

– Rich Winograd

Remember when exam time came around at the end of each semester of study? Most of us spent several nights before the event cramming from notes and textbooks. It was a stressful time and did little to add to our prolonged learning.

Learning transpires best moment by moment, hour by hour, and not as an afterthought that calculates into a final grade. I suspect life is like that too. I wonder what happens at our end time when we hurry to actualize many of our dreams before it is really too late? When the clock runs down do we run out and hurry to do what we delayed in doing during our allotted time here? Practically speaking, that probably doesn't happen due to age and energy loss. But, it is good to consider because right now if we are able-bodied and healthy we are capable of actualizing whatever it is we want to do.

This week we will be on Action Assignment #2. I hope that you did #1 this past week, and are now prepared for the new challenge. Remember, the purpose of these activities is to prime the pump and not to be a stand in for what you want to do. In the beginning it can take a little coaching before you muster up your own personal initiative. It's easy once someone shows you how. And, with the "why" in place, the "how" is always just a mechanism to get you moving toward your destiny.

So, with that being said, in the famous words of W. Clement Stone, "Do It NOW!"

Know Your Own Mind, Live Your Own Life

by Napoleon Hill

Somewhere along the path of life, every successful man finds out how to live his own life as he wishes to live it.

The younger you are when you discover this mighty power, the more likely you are to live successfully and happily. Yet even in later years, many make the great change—from letting others make them what they are, to making sure that they make their lives to their own liking.

The Creator gave man the prerogative of power over his own mind. It must have been the Creator's purpose to encourage man to live his own life, think his own thoughts, find his own goals and achieve them. Simply by exercising this profound prerogative you can bring abundance into your life, and with it know the greatest wealth of all, peace of mind, without which there can be no real happiness.

Grow Rich With Peace of Mind. Fawcett Books, 1967, p. 1.

Action Assignment #2

Design your personal coat of arms. Read the story below for inspiration. Next, decide what to put on your coat of arms. Now, however you choose, design your coat of arms that bears a single image and a single descriptive word.

In a speech made years ago, James J. Davis, then Secretary of State, said: "The beaver is a builder and the rat is a destroyer, yet they both belong to the rodent race. The beaver harvests his food in the summer, he builds a house and stores that food for winter. The rat sneaks to the food stores of others; he eats what he wants, ruins the rest, and then runs and hides in his hole. He lives in the builder's house, but he is not the builder. He undermines that house; he is a rat.

"Some men are by nature beavers, and some are rats; yet they all belong to the human race. A civilization rises when the beaver-men outnumber the rat-men. When the rat-men get the upper hand then civilization falls. Then the rats turn and eat one another and that is the end. Beware of breeding rats in America."

Chapter 3

You, I, and almost everyone can do something about the phenomenon of mind pollution. And it's not costly to anyone—except for the profits that will be lost by those who pollute minds..

– W. Clement Stone

This week I would like to continue our action challenge by having you consider how awake and aware you really are. By being bold and remaining awake even when you are constantly sedated by the common place things of life, you control your destiny. By being a participant and not an observer you enable yourself to garner unseen wealth and riches at first through the actions that you take. Knowing that it is in doing that others achieve greatness, you begin to condition yourself to become a "doer."

What, you may ask, is it that I am supposed to do? Never mind. Just be ready and willing to undertake whatever opportunities avail themselves to you. If you weigh the opportunity with caution, doubt, criticism, and potential worthiness, chances are it will pass you by. However, if you accept the hidden gift buried in the mundane, you will find that with each opportunity the end result grows in proportion to your acceptance of the gift. Sounds subtle, and it is. The gift does not arrive on your doorstep in full bloom with a red ribbon attached accompanied by an embossed greeting card that wishes you everlasting health, wealth, and happiness. Rather, it arrives as a seed, a bit of nothing, that has the potential to create beauty beyond compare if at first you plant it, nurture it, tend it, and cultivate it. Sounds like work, right? It is. But anything worth having is worth working for ultimately.

It has been said that if we have a desire for a certain achievement, that desire would not have been placed within us without the accompanying potential to achieve it. Nature never gives us the dream without the means to accomplish it. That's amazing because we never need say, "I can't." It is in accepting the dream and resting assured that divine intervention will lead us to the best possible outcome that the dream can be fulfilled. A dream resisted or declined ends up haunting us or nagging at our heart because it never materialized. Only you can give it life.

So, this week stay awake to your potential. It is truly unlimited. Do not be lulled into complacency. Risk the joy of knowing that you are fully alive and capable of doing that which you set your heart on accomplishing. Be the cause of great happenings. You hold the key to your success.

Your Beginning

by Napoleon Hill

You will come to the point, sooner or later, at which you will want to do something bigger and better than you have ever done before. When you do, you are going to be discouraged by those around you who know you best, and who will say the plan you have is foolish or beyond your power to carry out. You will find more people willing to tear you down by discouragement than you will find sympathizing with you and helping you to build your ego. The best way to avoid such discouragement is to confide only in those who have a genuine sympathy with your cause and an understanding of your possibilities. Otherwise, keep your plans to yourself and let your actions speak. Adopt the motto Deeds—Not Words. It is a good motto for everyone.

It may not be in the best taste for you to overestimate your abilities, but it is better than to underestimate, and it will do less harm. If you aim at a very big achievement and attain only a moderate achievement, you will still have attained something. If you allow yourself to be held back before you even begin, you will have sold yourself short and will attain nothing.

PMA Science of Success, Educational Edition. Napoleon Hill Foundation, 1961, p. 277.

Action Assignment #3

Read *That Something* by W. Woodbridge

Next, create two columns. In the left-hand column list 15 things that put you to sleep, or are counterproductive to the fulfillment of your immediate goals. In the corresponding right-hand column, list how you are going to fight off these mind numbing "sleeping agents" and remain fully awake.

CHAPTER 4

If you knew that what you are beginning would certainly do well, from the moment you begin till the moment of the work's ultimate reception, how would you feel? How would you act?

– Dorothea Brande

Have you ever been asked, "What is your MO?" This abbreviation for *modus operandi* refers to a technique or a manner of doing something. But, let's expand the definition to include the title of one of W. Clement Stone's favorite novels: *Magnificent Obsession* by Lloyd C. Douglas. To have an MO of this magnitude you have to have a world vision that is larger than yourself—a manner of giving yourself away for a cause which is greater than you are. In other words, something enduring that will exist beyond your own limited lifespan. In Napoleon Hill's terminology this could be your Definiteness of Purpose.

Hardly a week goes by without someone asking me how to find their DCA or definite chief aim in life. It is not an easy question to answer, but the source of your DCA is contained within your passion. By answering the question, "What am I passionate about?" you will begin to zero in on your target and eventually hit the bull's-eye. A clue is that it is something you willingly give to others because you find it rewarding even if you are not compensated monetarily for the time and talent you expend in delivering it.

Considering that you could spend your life on something that may not bring you immediate financial rewards, you might begin to envision another MO in the here and now. That would be you Magnificent Outcome. This MO is the best possible outcome that you foresee from your efforts that correlate with your Magnificent Obsession. This MO is the proverbial Pot of Gold at the end of the rainbow. Your reward for the life well lived on the road less taken. Envision it now, and then proceed to make this MO deliver on schedule.

Just think! If you can align the three MO's in your life—What you desire, how you will achieve it, and the positive outcome that you can expect to receive for staying the course, you will have mastered the only thing that matters—why you are on this planet in the first place.

Now, when someone asks you, "What's your MO?" you can rest assured that they are asking you to define more than a method of doing something, but rather engaging the very Socratic method of helping you figure out your reason for being.

Our Matchless System of Free Enterprise

by Napoleon Hill

Our great American Way of Life, our matchless system of free enterprise, and the personal liberty of which we feel so proud, are nothing more than the mental attitude of people organized and directed to specialized ends.

The one factor of the American Way of Life which stands out boldly above all others consists of the laws and the mechanisms of government we have set up to protect the individual in the freedom of control over his mental attitude.

It was this freedom of control over mental attitude which gave us the great leaders who patterned our American Way of Life and our great system of free enterprise. And it is significant that only those who moved with a positive mental attitude became leaders.

Thomas A. Edison's positive mental attitude sustained him through more than ten thousand failures and led him to the discovery of the incandescent electric light which ushered in the great electrical age and the fabulous riches it gave us.

Henry Ford's positive mental attitude kept him afloat during his early struggles in building his first automobile, and it served as his greatest and most important asset in establishing the monumental industrial empire, which made him richer than Croesus and provided employment, directly and indirectly, for perhaps more than ten million men and women.

Andrew Carnegie's positive mental attitude lifted him up from poverty and obscurity and served as his major asset in the establishment of an industry which gave birth to the great steel age, which now serves as the most important link in our entire economic system.

You Can Work Your Own Miracles. Fawcett Publishing, 1971, p. 16.

Action Assignment #4

Do a little investigative work. Meet your higher self by answering these three questions:

1. MO – Who am I? How do I define my Modus Operandi? What is my special calling? What are my talents and gifts that are unique to me?
2. MO – What is my Magnificent Obsession? What positive dream engages my mind, monopolizes my thoughts, and pushes me forward? What is it that I would do for the sole enjoyment of doing?
3. MO – How, when and where do I envision my Magnificent Outcome?

Now, step into your future this minute by beginning, right where you are, to take action on giving yourself away by engaging your special gift. Write down the results you notice, and mentally be grateful that you have the opportunity to be the only you there is in this entire Universe who can deliver that special gift.

Chapter 5

> *People usually don't* choose *to stop believing in themselves. It just happens, because lack of motivation and drive is easier than success.*
>
> – *Matthew "Matt Mic" Crawford*

Storytelling is a great way to learn a lesson. When the words "Once Upon a Time" are spoken, people anticipate a tale that will entertain as well as educate. A receptive mood creates an opportunity for learning to be fun and enjoyable. Stories about barnyard animals, fairies, heroes, beautiful maidens, ugly trolls, witches, and dragons frequently accompany youngsters to dreamland. The question "Do you want to hear a story?" is almost always answered in the affirmative.

Napoleon Hill knew that stories were good instructional tools. His works are filled with illustrative stories that drive his lessons home. In *Think and Grow Rich* and *Law of Success,* the reader is introduced to story after story that is the application of each principle in real life. Examples are cited, people are named, and the main idea is underscored with a story. The directive, tell a story—make a point, is Dr. Hill's favorite methodology in reaching the general reader.

Today, many of the historical figures Dr. Hill uses to bring home his point are unknown to young readers. That should not be a problem since the lesson of the story is what is more important. Does it really matter if we read about three pigs, three bears, or three raccoons if we understand the point of the story? No. What is significant is that the lesson in the story is as applicable today as it was 100 years ago.

Our brains are wired for stories. Recall is better when the lesson is imbedded in a story. New information is remembered in greater detail when we have a "hook" to hang it on to. The story is the "hook" that carries the lesson and enables us to recall it. Whether you are reading about Andrew Carnegie, Henry Ford, W. Clement Stone, the Wright Brothers, Thomas Edison, or any other famous personage, the purpose for reading about their life is in detailing the lessons of personal enterprise that lead to success.

So, the key to enrichment is in the story. When you resonate with a story you become inspired to do as the hero or heroine does and likewise achieve success in your special area of interest or calling. When you learn through the experience of others, you can save yourself the trouble of having to walk every step of the way yourself.

The Enchanted Kettle

by Napoleon Hill

Fifty years ago, an old country doctor drove to town, hitched his horse, quietly slipped into a drug store by the back door, and began "dickering" with the young drug clerk. His mission was destined to yield great wealth to many people. It was destined to bring to the South the most far-flung benefit since the Civil War.

For more than an hour, behind the prescription counter, the old doctor and the clerk talked in low tones. Then the doctor left. He went out to the buggy and brought back a large, old fashioned kettle. A big wooden paddle (used for stirring the contents of the kettle), and deposited them in the back of the store.

The clerk inspected the kettle, reached into his inside pocket, took out a roll of bills, and handed it over to the doctor. The roll contained exactly $500.00—the clerk's entire savings!

The doctor handed over a small slip of paper on which was written a secret formula. The words on that small slip of paper were worth a King's ransom! But not to the doctor! Those magic words were needed to start the kettle to boiling, but neither the doctor nor the young clerk knew what fabulous fortunes were destined to flow from that kettle.

The old doctor was glad to sell the outfit for five hundred dollars. The money would pay off his debts, and give him freedom of mind. The clerk was taking a big chance by staking his entire life's savings on a mere scrap of paper and an old kettle! He never dreamed his investment would start a kettle to over-flowing with gold that would surpass the miraculous performance of Aladdin's lamp.

What the clerk really purchased was an IDEA!

Think and Grow Rich. The Ralston Society, 1937, pp. 132–133.

Action Assignment #5

Share with another person the benefits that you have experienced by reading and applying the teachings of Napoleon Hill. Tell a story. Make a point. Deliver the message, and note the result. You could be giving the single best gift to an individual that they have ever received in their lifetime. Tell a simple, direct, and informational story to one other person. Be sincere and grateful. Give freely and unconditionally for the enhancement of another person's life. As Gandhi said: "Be the change you want to see in the world." Change for good, right now, yourself, by making the world a better place by telling your story.

Chapter 6

It seems, in fact, as though the second half of a man's life is made up of nothing, but the habits he has accumulated during the first half.
– Fyodor Dostoevsky

Do you ever feel that you can predict the future? Just as the Groundhog forecasts an early spring or six more weeks of winter based upon whether or not it sees its shadow, you too can foresee many outcomes in your life and the lives of others based upon the examination of personal habits.

Dr. Hill states that Cosmic Habitforce is the comptroller of the Universe and is the plan put in place by the Creator that keeps things orderly. The more a person operates within this system, the greater the opportunity for success. All people are born equal under this system meaning that each person can decide to cultivate positive or negative habits. Both good and bad habits once formed become fixations and these fixations are carried out automatically. In other words, a person whose habits are entrenched operates on autopilot. This can be either a good or bad thing depending upon the nature of a person's automatic habits. If required, a great deal of will power and self-discipline is essential to clear existing habits.

Habits, once cultivated, become rote. Like the recitation of the alphabet and the multiplication tables, little brain power is involved in recalling these lists once learned. So too, laziness or personal initiative, poverty consciousness or wealth consciousness, aimless drifting or definiteness of purpose, and a host of countless other habits of thought and action can lodge in our minds like groves in an old-fashioned record recording. When played out in our life, the habitual groove of the recorded piece plays out the result of the positive or negative traits performed day by day.

What song will be your theme song? One of riches, or one of poverty? Your habits determine the score.

Why Straight Thinking is Such a Rarity

by Napoleon Hill

Two great forces are working in the minds of all men to make them what they are. One is social heredity, and the other is physical heredity.

Physical heredity is the law of nature through which the sum and substance of all characteristics, traits and physical aspects of your ancestors, through the ages, have been handed on to you. You are unavoidably a product of all your ancestors.

Social heredity consists of every influence with which you will come in contact, from the time you reach a state of consciousness until you die. Your mother's and father's influence, your education, the conversations you listen to, religious influences, political ideas, the newspapers you read, the shows you see – they all have and will help to make you what you are. They are your social inheritance. Very few persons have what it takes to pull away from these and do some independent, accurate thinking for themselves. A few cast off their social inheritance and dare to be different and individualistic. When this happens, the world has an Edison, a Ford, a Thomas Paine, an Ingersoll or a Jonas Salk. But the vast majority of people allow themselves to become victims of social heredity. This is why straight thinking is such a rarity.

PMA Science of Success, Educational Edition. Napoleon Hill Foundation, 1961, pp. 504–505.

Action Assignment #6

Select two role models — one from your physical heredity and one from your social heredity. Display a photo of each person and consciously state what aspect of their personality you want to emulate in your life. What positive habits can you extract from their lives and how can you "borrow" these same habits and make them your own? Next, see if you can trace the invisible but very real power of Cosmic Habitforce in each of their lives.

Chapter 7

It is in giving that we receive, it is in pardoning that we are pardoned, and it is in dying that we are born to eternal life.
– St. Francis of Assisi

How can I be of service? This question can be a tough one because the first thing we think about is joining the Peace Corps, becoming a missionary, or running a soup kitchen. But, isn't this just an excuse that keeps us from doing something that we can really manage right now, today? If our service must be something that we can brag about to elevate our status, is it really a service or a self-serving plot to impress or boost our sense of self-worth? I would like to suggest that if we have to think about what is worthy of our service then we are missing the point.

Listening instead of speaking; entertaining instead of being entertained; doing a chore instead of hiring it done; asking "how can I help you?" instead of asking "can you do this for me?"; working overtime instead of taking time off; and multiple other things that we would prefer not to do but can always be of service by doing are mentioned for everyone to consider. Washing the car, doing the dishes, answering the phone, sweeping the floor, doing the laundry, making the bed, cooking dinner, and on and on are all ways of service. Get the point? We do not have to cross over our own doorstep to be of service. Opportunities are abounding, but those who report for duty are rare.

Little actions taken over time create profound lifetime habits that determine our destiny. If you can't see this coming, then you do not understand Cosmic Habitforce as Dr. Hill describes it. Through our simple daily actions we ourselves create the patterns that become automatic through repetition in our lives. These automatic habits eventually determine our pleasing (or not so pleasing) personality traits. Thought habits and mental attitudes go hand in glove with these actions.

Make it your highest intention to cultivate good habits. When you do, you will be rewarded by the potential that you create for yourself.

Habits are the Stairway to a Richer Life

by Napoleon Hill

You can see that an oak tree grows from an acorn, always, and a pine tree grows from the seed of its ancestor. And you know that Nature never makes a mistake and grows a pine tree from an acorn, nor an oak tree from the seed of a pine.

There are facts you can see. But do you recognize that they do not "just happen" by chance—something has to make them happen! That something is the power which fixes habits and makes them permanent. Man is the only creature which the Creator permits the privilege of fixing his own habits to suit his own desires.

We are ruled by habits, all of us! Our habits are fastened upon us by repetition of our thoughts and acts. Therefore we can control our earthly destinies and our way of living only to the extent that we control our thoughts. We must direct them to form the sort of habits we need to serve as our road map to guide our lives. Good habits which lead to success can be ordered and used by any individual. Bad habits can be broken and replaced by good ones at will by anyone.

Man Has Control

The habits of every living creature except man are fixed by what we call "instinct." This places them under limitations from which they cannot escape.

The Creator not only gave men complete, unchallengeable control over the power of thought, but with this gift came the means of possessing thought power and directing it to any desired end.

The Creator has also given man another privilege whereby thoughts are made to clothe themselves in their physical likeness and equivalent.

Here, then, is a profound truth. With it you may open doors to wisdom and live an ordered life, you will be able to control those factors necessary to your success.

The rewards available to the person who takes possession of his own mind power and directs it to definite ends of his own choice are great in number. But penalties for not doing so are equally great in number.

Miami Herald. Science of Success Series. June 1, 1956.

Action Assignment #7

Read this poem by St. Francis of Assisi:

Lord, make me an instrument of Thy peace;
where there is hatred, let me sow love;
where there is injury, pardon;
where there is doubt, faith;
where there is despair, hope;
where there is darkness, light;
and where there is sadness, joy.

O Divine Master,
grant that I may not so much seek to be consoled as to console;
to be understood, as to understand;
to be loved, as to love;
for it is in giving that we receive,
it is in pardoning that we are pardoned,
and it is in dying that we are born to eternal life.

Notice that there are six calls to action in the first half of the poem. Read each step below. Next to the statement, indicate how you will do this in an observable and measurable way this week.

1. where there is hatred, let me sow love; What I will do . . . .
2. where there is injury, pardon; What I will do . . . .
3. where there is doubt, faith; What I will do . . . .
4. where there is despair, hope; What I will do . . . .
5. where there is darkness, light; What I will do . . . .
6. and where there is sadness, joy. What I will do . . . .

Now, this is your assignment. You must take the abstract thought and turn it into a concrete action. For example, in sowing love to counteract hatred, you might apologize to someone for something you did that hurt them. The apology should be written or verbal, not merely something you think about. Follow through in each of the six points with what you said you would do. Record your results after you have completed each step. Notice how your habits of action are now creating the life you choose to live one step at a time.

Chapter 8

Knute Rockne, famous coach at Notre Dame, knew the value of suggestion and used it repeatedly. But he always suited his method of applying it to the temperament of the individual team.

– Claude M. Bristol

Whether it's because of all the focus on "green living" or simply the fact that I am a pack rat, before throwing things away I ask myself how I can re-purpose the item. Somehow, when I ask myself if there is another way that I can put an item to a different use it stirs my creativity and leaves me with less of a guilty conscience for adding to the landfills.

Using the concept of "found art" I look for things that I can use in my garden to serve as trellises or yard decorations. When my lights no longer worked on my outdoor Holiday Reindeer, I removed them and created topiary-like arrangements that my plants love to climb.

I have been collecting large wine jugs too for some time, thinking that they would make wonderful centerpieces for summer tables both indoors and out, but I was unsure how to use them. Last weekend I visited a store and noticed a new product. The bottoms of glass wine bottles were cut away and tea lights were displayed inside. They were beautiful and served as protection for the candles to stay lit.

Years ago I can still recall how my friend's mother salvaged clear bottles and filled them with colored water and displayed them on the top rim of her kitchen cabinets. When the light reflected just right the bottles cast rainbow rays of color into her room. She managed to brighten her days in an almost cost free fashion.

As I think about re-purposing, I also think about how lessons from decades ago can be made new. The spark of truth or the kernel of wisdom is still inside the story, but to get the point across to a younger audience the story may need to be updated. As I read Napoleon Hill's works and review the stories that he relates, I know that because of his inherent wisdom there are modern counterparts. As you read *Think and Grow Rich* or *Law of Success*, you might just ask yourself how best you can integrate and apply the very same lessons today in your life and in the lives of those who will come after you.

As the saying goes, you do not have to reinvent the wheel to use it. You just have to remember that the center of the wheel, the hub, remains constant. The spokes of the wheel can represent your own creativity and inspiration in passing the lessons along to future generations of Napoleon Hill students.

The Magic Plan

by Napoleon Hill

"A man cannot directly choose his circumstances, but he can choose his thoughts, and so indirectly, yet surely, shape his circumstances."

As surely as the sun rises in the East and sets in the West, here is a plan that will transform your personality into whatever you wish it to be:

Place this page on the walls of your room. Each night before you retire, relax, shut out all other thoughts and repeat the following, with firm determination to build it into your character, keeping your eyes fixed upon the picture of each character as you repeat the words which indicate the qualities you wish to build by emulating that character:

ABRAHAM LINCOLN: As I look upon your face I definitely pledge my earnest efforts to develop in my own character those qualities of patience, tolerance and love for all humanity, the weak and the strong, friend and foe, which were your distinguishing marks. I will emulate your example by looking for the good there is in others and by developing a love for justice.

RALPH WALDO EMERSON: As I look upon your face I resolve to develop in my own character those qualities which helped you to leave your footprints on the sands of time, namely, the ability to read the handwriting of Nature, as it is written in the faces of men, in flowing brooks, in the flowers, in growing trees, in the singing birds, in the faces of little children and in the rocks of prison walls.

ELBERT HUBBARD: As I look upon your face I resolve to develop in my own character that rare ability, that was your distinguishing mark, to state my conclusions in words that vibrate with life, action and enthusiasm.

GEORGE WASHINGTON: As I look upon your face I resolve to develop courage and the persistence with which to complete all that I undertake.

NAPOLEON BONAPARTE: As I look upon your face I resolve to develop the strategic ability to lay hold of the organized forces that are available for my use, and to develop the self-confidence to master all handicaps which come my way. You shall serve as a constant reminder that the quitter never wins; that eternal vigilance and the courage to carry on in spite of every obstacle are the price of success.

____

(Sign here)

"Dream lofty dreams,
and as you Dream,
so shall you become.
Your Vision is the promise
of what you Shall one day be;
your Ideal is the Prophecy
of what you shall at last Unveil."
– *Allen*

Napoleon Hill's Magazine. September, 1921.

Action Assignment #8

Consider Napoleon's Hill's philosophy as a wheel with 17 spokes – each spoke representing a principle of success.

For each spoke, detail a new role model for the classic lesson that Dr. Hill teaches. For example, on the spoke labeled "Going the Extra Mile" ask yourself who you know today that would be an example of a person who continually goes the extra mile for someone else. This person does not have to be a celebrity or a recognized "name." He/she could be a neighbor, parent, teacher, friend, boss, minister, or relative, who has honed this characteristic to perfection. Match each principle to one current model of success who performs well for the principle under consideration.

Chapter 9

> *It is impossible to think of two things at once, that is to say that two ideas may be in juxtaposition, but they cannot be superimposed in our mind.*
>
> – *Émile Coué*

Recently I was visiting a friend at her new residence and saw a sign in the hallway that pointed to "Mission Integration." Having never seen a place quite like that, I mulled over what people would find at that location. My mind immediately jumped to Dr. Hill's success philosophy and I considered what a valuable service a mission integration room could offer. If people could just integrate their definite major purpose (mission) in life with their mental, spiritual, social, emotional, physical, and financial areas of their existence wouldn't they experience an even broader application of what they are placed here to do? I think so.

Using the analogy of a necklace, I would like you to consider each pearl. Singly, pearls placed on a table side by side might be compared to individual aspects of our life—one pearl at a time. These pearls could easily be scattered on the table, fall on the floor, and get lost very quickly. Without a unifying chain holding them together it matters little how pretty they look placed singly for everyone to see. However, the real beauty occurs when each pearl is strung together forming a beautiful necklace that can be worn and admired. That's Mission Integration.

Unless each of our actions in alignment with our definite major purpose is integrated for a cohesive purpose, it matters little what a person does day in and day out. Just as beads in a box scatter everywhere when dropped, so too a life without a unified purpose does little in accomplishing anything of worth.

In integrating your mission in life obviously you need to choose good pearls to connect together on your journey. As you consider the many aspects of self that each of us has to work with, why not look at the larger picture and remind yourself daily that all that you do needs to work together to achieve the common good of your mission. Ask yourself if your action is a pearl of great value and worthy of a spot adorning your gold chain? This simple analogy will help you better select what you want to do with the time and opportunities that each of us is given.

A Powerful Form of Energy

by Napoleon Hill

No one knows what thought is, but every philosopher and every man of scientific ability who has given any study to the subject is in accord with the statement that thought is a powerful form of energy which directs the activities of the human body; that every idea held in the mind through prolonged, concentrated thought, takes on permanent form and continues to affect the bodily activities according to its nature, either consciously or unconsciously.

Auto-suggestion, which is nothing more or less than an idea held in the mind, through thought, is the only known principle through which one may literally make himself over, after any pattern he may choose.

Napoleon Hill's Magazine. July, 1921, p. 23.

Action Assignment #9

Consider your daily actions as deeds that will comprise the beads forming your mission necklace.

Select several different types of beads. Large, gaudy beads, sparkling beads, colorful beads, beads of varying shapes, tarnished beads, broken beads, etc. You get the idea. Place the beads in a container and as you progress throughout your day by taking actions, select a bead for each major action you complete. You might consider doing this by writing out a to-do list first daily of 10 items per day for a total of 70 per week.

As you complete each action on your to-do list, select a bead that represents each action and the degree to which it was in alignment with your mission. Begin to actually construct your necklace. How does it look? Will it be something that could be sold at Tiffany's or on a bargain basement closeout table? Notice that you are the creator and you control the outcome of the beads and the necklace. As your necklace takes shape you can see the visible results of your commitment to your life's mission, one bead at a time.

CHAPTER 10

Pick out one bad habit. Do you own it, lock, stock and barrel? Is it your personal property? Are you proud of it? Really, isn't it a liability? Why not turn it into an asset by supplanting it with a good habit?
– William H. Danforth

Matthew Arnold wrote that "the seeds of God-like power are in us still." Let's get imaginative and wonder how many inspirational words are in a new pen, how many world changing actions are in a book, how many flowers are in a seed, how much love is in a love note, how many gourmet dinners are in a new pot, and how many best-selling novels are in the unmarked notebook?

Seeds of greatness always exist before the outcome. The wonder in this is that the very seeds of greatness that reside within each of us may incubate, germinate, sprout, grow, and produce exactly as we envision them doing, or they may wither right before our eyes and die on the vine. What causes the different outcomes when the source of power is the same? The answer is simple. We do.

Our actions align with the seeds of power that we cultivate, and the outgrowth is what we deliver to the world. This gift of greatness works best when our good habits are in alignment with the source that enabled us to think the thought.

Dr. Hill states in Chapter 1, Introduction, to *Think and Grow Rich* that: "Truly, 'thoughts are things,' and powerful things at that, when they are mixed with definiteness of purpose, persistence, and a BURNING DESIRE for their translation into riches or other material objects."

If there is magic in the above formula it is that the power for the translation of thoughts into riches always resides within us. It is located dead center in the seeds of God-like power that reside in each of us. Our job is to bring these forth and provide a nurturing environment where they can grow and produce the outcomes we desire. But simply planting the seeds is insufficient. We have to care for the seeds and tend to the plants as they mature before we can enjoy the fruits of our labor. This cycle works best when first we cultivate good habits that pre-determine positive outcomes. As Hill states, it takes persistence and hard work before an idea is born. Will you be a good idea parent?

It all depends on you.

My Dominant Thoughts

by Napoleon Hill

I have never been accused of being overly credulous or superstitious. I have never been impressed very much by so-called miracles, but I am compelled to admit that I have seen the working out, in my own evolution during the past twenty odd years, certain principles which have produced seemingly miraculous results. I have watched the development and unfoldment of my own mind, and while I ordinarily am not very deeply impressed by any "miracle" the cause of which I cannot trace, I must admit that much has happened in the development of my own mind which I cannot trace back to original cause.

This much I do know, however; I know that my outward, bodily action invariably harmonizes with and corresponds to the nature of the thoughts which dominate my mind; the thoughts which I permit to drift into my mind, or those which I deliberately place there with the intention of giving them domination over my bodily activities.

My own experience has proved conclusively that character need not be a matter of chance! Character can be built to order just the same as a house can be built to correspond to a set of previously drawn up plans. My own experience has proved conclusively that a man can rebuild his character in a remarkable short length of time, ranging all the way from a few weeks to a few years, depending upon the determination and the desire with which he goes at the task.

Napoleon Hill's Magazine. July, 1921, pp. 27–28.

Action Assignment #10

Character development begins personally when one desires to change designated characteristics that have become unproductive habits. Take twenty minutes today to acknowledge ten bad habits that you choose to rebuild into good habits. List the bad habit first and then the transformative good habit. You might list something like:

1. Snack food junkie – healthy choices in snacks
2. Procrastinator – a doer and a completer
3. Downgrades others – compliments others
4. Unlimited T.V. time – reads 30 minutes per day

Get the idea? Only you can change your performance by modifying one bad habit at a time. It will make a difference in the pleasing personality you grow for the good of yourself and others.

CHAPTER 11

When you meet a person who has complimentary statements to say regarding everyone—does that person look small in your eyes? To the contrary, you look at him as a genuinely big person.
– Ben Sweetland

Dr. Hill reminds us that habits are first cobwebs than cables. Habits begin with thought. Positive habits develop due to right thinking and negative habits develop due to wrong thinking. By using self-discipline right now, we can control any negativity that might be seeping into our consciousness. As any good gardener will tell you, the best time to weed is when the plants are young and easily uprooted. Left untended, our garden will soon be overrun with weeds and produce little that is eatable.

When our mind garden is weed free, it is a good time to acknowledge this positive frame of mind and continue to work toward expanding this awareness. One way to do this is to become a "good-finder." By focusing on the positive rather than the negative, the formation of good habits is occurring. By looking for something to praise rather than something to complain about we will soon find more riches arriving in abundance. By uncovering previously hidden riches we are now capable of finding even more and bringing them home to harvest. This is the master key in creating a true millionaire's lifestyle. No amount of money in the world can buy you the joy and happiness you will accumulate when you think positively and cultivate the habit of right thinking.

Remember, our thoughts shape our world and, in turn, shape our earthly destiny. If we choose the right road rather than the wrong one, not only will we arrive earlier than most but we will arrive in a better frame of mind. Think positively.

The 12 Riches of Life

by Napoleon Hill

1. A Positive Mental Attitude
2. Sound Physical Health
3. Harmony in Human Relationships
4. Freedom from Fear
5. The Hope of Achievement
6. The Capacity for Faith
7. Willingness to Share One's Blessings
8. A Labor of Love
9. An Open Mind on All Subjects
10. Self-Discipline
11. The Capacity to Understand People
12. Financial Security

We can become complete masters of ourselves, if we so desire. The main thought to bear in mind is first to gain the knowledge, and secondly to apply it.

You Can Work Your Own Miracles. Fawcett Books/Random House, 1996, pp. 79–85.

Action Assignment #11

Review the 12 Riches of Life that Napoleon Hill lists above.

In your notebook, find five examples for each of the twelve riches in your own life. By doing this, you are unearthing your personal treasure that already exists in your life even if it has been buried or hidden for a time. Next, using the same 12 Riches of Life, indicate how you are going to bring this richness into someone else's life.

As you acknowledge your gifts, and then decide to help others attain these very same gifts, you are bestowing upon yourself a double blessing. By helping others you also expand your range of power, and simultaneously that bestows a blessing on you that makes you happy. Finally, do it now. Once completed, the incurred blessings will be priceless!

Chapter 12

To believe in bad luck is a beautiful excuse for failure. It is a perfect defense against hard work. If you have a premonition that you are going to fail in an undertaking, you are promising yourself disaster in advance.

– *George Harrison Phelps*

More often than we would like to admit each of us falls prey to one or more of the seven negative emotions. When our PMA levels recede correspondingly our NMA levels rise. This reversal is accompanied by a great backlash of negative emotions. Fear, Jealousy, Hatred, Revenge, Greed, Superstition, and Anger all begin to take possession of our waking and sleeping hours and soon all of our energy is spent in getting even with someone for a perceived slight or worse. Rather than focusing on the good that we can do, we focus on the hatred that we can create. Some call this human nature, but is it really human or is it sub-human?

In sliding into the NMA side of thinking we begin to foster negative thoughts that blacken our world. Ask yourself the following questions:

- Am I fearful or faithful?
- Am I jealous or trusting?
- Am I hateful or loving?
- Am I revengeful or forgiving?
- Am I greedy or giving?
- Am I superstitious or optimistic?
- Am I angry or even tempered?

As you consider each question, feel the emotion that wells up inside of you that precedes an action. If the action is based on the seven negative emotions, you harm yourself as you harm another. If the action is based on the corresponding positive emotions, you bless yourself as you care for another. So it is true. These emotions are double-edged swords. What we mete out to another, we also receive ourselves. Bad or good—it all emanates from us.

Today, when you begin to drift to the NMA side of the river of life, remind yourself that you want to only connect with what is on the PMA side of this river for the good of yourself and the good of others. Consciously, turn around your thoughts and move them in the PMA direction. You can do this consciously. It takes practice, persistence, and patience, but soon it will become a habit. And, for your own best interest, this is one habit that you want to cultivate..

The Seven Major Negative Emotions (To Be Avoided)

by Napoleon Hill

The emotion of FEAR
The emotion of JEALOUSY
The emotion of HATRED
The emotion of REVENGE
The emotion of GREED
The emotion of SUPERSTITION
The emotion of ANGER

Positive and negative emotions cannot occupy the mind at the same time. One or the other must dominate. It is your responsibility to make sure that positive emotions constitute the dominating influence of your mind. Here the law of HABIT will come to your aid. Form the habit of applying and using the positive emotions! Eventually, they will dominate your mind so completely, that the negatives cannot enter it.

Think and Grow Rich. The Ralston Society, 1937, pp. 297–298.

Action Assignment #12

Consider the seven negative emotions listed above. For each emotion, reflect on a circumstance in your own life when you allowed the negative emotion to grab hold of you. What was the outcome? How did you feel afterwards? What did you do next due to the outcome? How do you feel about this occurrence today? What lesson did you learn?

Next, do the same thing in reverse for the corresponding positive emotions. Repeat this exercise until you are convinced that you control the outcome — positive or negative — that you want to create in your life one thought at a time.

Chapter 13

Going the extra mile is a priceless concept because I believe all of the great things in life can be discovered within that proverbial extra mile. Many people miss the power of this concept because they are waiting to go the extra mile until they get into their chosen field or the area of life where they are hoping to be successful.

– Jim Stovall

As I listened to the readings in church yesterday, I was struck by the statement, "They stood and watched and did nothing." The thought comes to mind that we are not meant to be spectators in life, but participants. How often do we stand, watch, and do nothing? It makes a person wonder as to why things may go awry when we fail to take action. Worse yet, those who fail to take action often wonder out loud, "Well, why doesn't somebody do something?" Consider the fact that you may be just that somebody who was sent to act.

Failure to act can often be blamed on low self-esteem, lack of self-confidence, fear of reprisals, fear of criticism, fear of being laughed at, and worrying about any scenario that could "maybe" happen.

Napoleon Hill states in *Think and Grow Rich* that, "Without doubt, the most common weakness of all human beings is the habit of leaving their minds open to the negative influence of other people." Consider for a moment how often you have failed to speak up, passed up a chance to be heard, or failed to make a contribution because you felt someone knew more about a particular situation than you did. Therefore, your voice was throttled just as surely as if someone grabbed you by the throat and choked you, you became speechless, and as a direct consequence you failed to be heard.

So, now, let's make a new rule. The old one is still good advice—Don't speak out of turn. But, let's add another part—Don't speak out of turn. *Wait your turn, and then speak!* When it is your turn, deliver your message, and then act with the courage of your convictions.

If you are given a voice, remember to use it when you have something valuable to say. By withholding your commentary, you negate your contribution. Everybody is gifted, and your gift may be just the one that the world needs to receive in order to make the world a better place in which to live one thoughtful and worthy contribution at a time.

Absolute Control

by Napoleon Hill

You have ABSOLUTE CONTROL over but one thing and that is your thoughts. This is the most significant and inspiring of all facts known to man! It reflects man's Divine nature. This Divine prerogative is the sole means by which you may control your own destiny. If you fail to control your own mind, you may be sure you will control nothing else.

If you must be careless with your possessions, let it be in connection with material things. Your mind is your spiritual estate! Protect and use it with the care to which Divine Royalty is entitled. You were given a WILL-POWER for this purpose.

Unfortunately, there is no legal protection against those who, either by design or ignorance, poison the minds of others by negative suggestion. This form of destruction should be punishable by heavy legal penalties, because it may and often does destroy one's chances of acquiring material things which are protected by law.

Think and Grow Rich. The Ralston Society, 1937, pp. 367–368.

Action Assignment #13

Make a commitment to share your beliefs several times this week.

Do not simply stand, watch and do nothing. If someone takes you to task for what inspires you to talk and take action, this is good because you can give them the opportunity to share their own point of view too. A dialogue can begin and perhaps one or both of your worldviews might change for the better. Next, this can lead to constructive action. Any and all controversial subjects can be accessed by simply looking at news media sites. Zero in on one or two topics, say your peace and walk your talk. If you fail to stand up and be counted, then you shortchange yourself and fail the world.

Chapter 14

All that is necessary to break the spell of inertia and frustration is this: Act as if it were impossible to fail.

– Dorothea Brande

A German proverb states: God gives us the nuts, but he does not crack them. This is in alignment with the saying that God provides food for the birds of the air, but does not throw it into their nests! These thoughts almost certainly make one chuckle and nod in accord, but let me ask you, when the going gets tough do you get going? Most throw in the towel, stay in the nest, or lose the nutcracker! According to Napoleon Hill only 2% of the earth's population ever achieves their deepest desires because they drop out before they drop everything and focus on procurement of the desired result via self-discipline.

Self-discipline is one principle of Dr. Hill's Science of Success system that everyone understands but few emulate. It's easy to pinpoint the problem as a lack of self-discipline, but it is far harder to resolve the problem through personalized action.

For example, hardly anyone will deny that exercise is good for a person, but how often do people really participate in becoming and remaining active? It's not in knowing what is good for a person, but rather in the doing that counts. This applies to all parts of the human experience, not just in the physical nature of it. Body, mind, and spirit all need to be disciplined in order to mature and grow. Simply focusing on one aspect of ourselves is insufficient.

I like to focus on the various aspects of personhood that include the Mental, Physical, Financial, Social, Spiritual, and Emotional. By seeking balance in these critical areas, a person is able to round out his wheel of life so to speak and keep it rolling toward a desired destination. When one area becomes expanded and another is neglected, a person does not acquire a well-rounded personality that contributes to success. Perhaps mental enhancement is neglected for physical beauty. The person under consideration may exercise for an hour every single day, but fail to read a book a year. This lopsided lifestyle does not enhance a person's chances for success. Benjamin Franklin states "moderation in all things." And, moderation with balance is an even greater success determiner.

With the new season upon us, why not strive to seek balance in your life. You can read a book, exercise, make a new friend, review your finances, pray for guidance, and keep your emotions in check all in a day's time. By focusing on the facets of your personality as you would the facets of a diamond, you can only enhance the sparkle. Note too that when looking at a chandelier, you notice the light that is burned out and not the ones that are illuminated. Likewise, the same is true with your personality. In order to shine, you must have all those facets sparkle and all the bulbs lit.

The Secret of Getting Things Done

by W. Clement Stone & Napoleon Hill

How do you make the secret of getting things done a part of your life? By habit. And you develop habit through repetition. "Sow an action and you reap a habit; sow a habit and you reap a character; sow a character and you reap a destiny," said the great psychologist and philosopher William James. He was saying that you are what your habits make you. And you can choose your habits. You can develop any habit you wish when you use the self-starter.

Now what is the secret of getting things done and what is the self-starter that forces you to use this great secret?

The secret of getting things done is to act. The self-starter is the self-motivator DO IT NOW!

As long as you live, never say to yourself, "DO IT NOW!" unless you follow through with desirable action. Whenever action is desirable and the symbol DO IT NOW! flashes from your subconscious mind to your conscious mind, immediately act.

Make it a practice to respond to the self-starter DO IT NOW! in little things. You will quickly develop the habit of a reflex response so powerful that in times of emergency or when opportunity presents itself, you will act.

Success Through a Positive Mental Attitude. Prentice-Hall, Inc., 1960, p. 93.

Action Assignment #14

Begin taking immediate action for the Science of Success principles by concentrating on one principle for an entire week. Create a page for each of the principles. You will have 17 total pages, and the project will last for 17 weeks.

Across the top of each page, list the days of the week. Down the side, list the 17 principles. At the very top, place the principle you are concentrating on for the week. Mark with a little black dot each time you intentionally took action on the principle given the command "Do It Now." This will tell you at the end of each week how you use the 17 success principles in unison to achieve your goals in life. It will be revealed which principles you focus on the most, and which you need to use more often. When the series is complete after 17 successive weeks, begin again. This will encourage you to formulate good habits, and reduce the bad ones.

Chapter 15

To everything there is a season, a time for every purpose under the sun.

– Ecclesiastes

Springtime is the season for new beginnings. The ground breaks through with life. Trees blossom, bulbs sprout, grass greens, blue skies linger, sunlight warms the earth, and the soft breeze touches our senses with a bit of nostalgia. Since time immemorial this ritual has prepared the earth's residents to begin again. This "something" that awakens inside us, encourages renewal.

Falling in love with life requires action not inertia. Getting outdoors and greeting the season head on with rake or spade in hand enables each one of us to feel as if we have made a contribution to the planet. In Indiana I anticipate the arrival of the pussy willows, the return of the robins, the scent of lilacs, the blossoming of the cherry trees, the sprouting of the peonies, and the smell the first time the grass is cut. And, I do not have to leave my home to experience any one of these. These are rituals of spring for me, and fill me with wonder.

Rituals create much needed patterns in our lives. They reverence the good things. By creating rituals in our families and work environments, we honor the people that fill our lives. Celebrating birthdays, holidays, landmark dates, special one-time occurrences and honors, as well as the more mundane things such as the first robin of the season, unite us as a group. Begin today by thinking which days in the calendar are special to you and why. Ask someone about their special dates too. Next, share your dates and remember them when the day arrives – not just for yourself, but for the other person too. I love the greeting card quote that states:

"Friends are angels who lift our feet when our own wings have trouble remembering how to fly."

Be an angel and lift someone's spirits by remembering for them when they forget! They will never forget you because of it!.

Law of Balance

by Napoleon Hill

Most of us may not feel a deep interest in the balancing of the stars and planets, but all of us do have a keen interest in the methods by which we may take full advantage of the great Law of Universal Balance in adjusting the circumstances affecting our individual lives so that they benefit us. The best way to secure benefits from this great law is, first, by taking possession of our power of thought and using it to relate ourselves to the circumstances we can control, in a manner favorable to ourselves; and second, to use this same power of thought to adjust ourselves beneficially to all the circumstances affecting our lives which we cannot control.

From this brief analysis of the Law of Balance we are heartened and encouraged by the observation that this law keeps everything throughout the universe in line with nature's established pattern and plan, except man – the only living creature with the power to deviate from the influence of this, and all other natural laws, if and when he chooses, and is willing to pay the price for his deviation.

If you are searching for the supreme secret of success in all human endeavors, here is a very suitable point at which to stop, ponder, meditate and think, with the hope that the small still voice which speaks from within may bless you with the knowledge you seek.

You Can Work Your Own Miracles. Fawcett, 1996, pp. 114–115.

Action Assignment #15

Begin a record today of dates that hold significance for you.

Add birthdays, anniversaries, special dates, etc. Next, share this calendar with someone else, and then ask for theirs. Online greeting card companies make this easier, but if you like the old handwritten approach, that is okay too. Just begin today to create a list and share it. Soon, each day of the year will be filled with "special dates" for you and for others that you can honor by sending an e-card or e-mail. Soon you will be closer to friends, family, and acquaintances because of your thoughtfulness and vice versa.

Don't forget about dates for those special people in your life who have passed on. You might call this their "feast day" and honor your ancestors, both friends and family, who have made a difference in your life, but recalling them on their special days and perhaps playing it forward by performing a good deed in their memory as well.

Chapter 16

Oh, I marked the first for another day!
Yet knowing how way leads on to way
I doubted if I should ever come back.

– Robert Frost

We have all heard the admonition growing up: Do not lie, cheat, or steal. This is good advice made better when we add to it the quote by Elbert Hubbard that states: "Live truth instead of professing it." The sum total of both thoughts is that action speaks a million times louder than any words. This truth is best revealed as we watch our children. They model our example. They do as we do and not as we say.

Carnegie refers to this as intentional honesty. This type of honesty is simply the plain and unadulterated truth that is not embellished by prevarication, colored by little white lies, fine-tuned by which way the wind blows, or embellished for the sake of expediency. Expediency usually refers to what's in it for me, rather than what's good for the whole. I bet you never realized that truth could be so deceptive, did you?

How do we uphold our end of the bargain in "telling the truth, the whole truth, and nothing but the truth?" Well, it's not as easy as it seems. To remind ourselves of this just watch the world go by on any social media site. Looking at these glimpses into a person's world one would believe that we all live in Garrison Keillor's Lake Wobegon "where all the women are strong, all the men are good looking, and all the children are above average." Unfortunately, this is not reality for the mainstream.

As we challenge ourselves to cultivate a keen sense of justice, perhaps it seeks us too as we draw near to our life's definite major purpose. By being honest, forthright, and dedicated to our life's mission we can then in turn cultivate the cooperation and support of others who are on the same path. Isn't it funny that when the student is ready, the teacher shows up? How often has this happened to you? Makes you wonder about the wonder of it all!

In closing, a friend of mine sent me this quote from Os Guinness: "The calling is the truth that God calls us to Himself so decisively that everything we are, everything we do, and everything we have is invested with a special devotion and dynamism lived out as a response to His summons and service." Good honest food for thought that I believe Napoleon Hill and Andrew Carnegie would endorse.

A Keen Sense of Justice

by Napoleon Hill

HILL: Perhaps, Mr. Carnegie, it would be well for you to define what you mean by justice.

CARNEGIE: Justice, as I use the term here, has reference to *intentional honesty!* Many people are honest for the sake of expediency, but their brand of honesty is so flexible that they can stretch it to fit any circumstance where their immediate interests can be best extended. It is not that brand of honesty we are analyzing. We are talking about deliberate honesty that is so rigidly adhered to that the individual is motivated by it under circumstances that may not be to his immediate benefit, the same as to those that promise the greatest possible reward.

HILL: Mr. Carnegie, would you care to name some of the more obvious practical benefits of a keen sense of justice?

CARNEGIE: It establishes the basis of confidence, without which no one can have an attractive personality.

It builds a fundamentally sincere and sound character which, of itself, is one of the greatest of all attracting forces.

It not only attracts people, but it offers opportunities for personal gain in one's occupation.

It gives one a feeling of self-reliance and self-respect.

It places one in a better and more understanding relationship with one's own conscience.

It attracts friends and discourages enemies.

It clears the way for that state of mind known as Faith.

It protects one from the destructiveness of controversies with other people.

It helps one to move with more initiative in connection with one's major purpose in life.

It never damages one nor does it subject one to any form of embarrassment.

A keen sense of justice not only aids in the development of attractive personality, but it is an asset of priceless value in almost every human relationship. It discourages avarice, greed, and selfishness, and gives an individual a much better understanding of his rights, privileges, and responsibilities. A keen sense of justice has a very definite and very great contributory influence in the development of the other traits of attractive personality.

The Wisdom of Andrew Carnegie as Told to Napoleon Hill. The Napoleon Hill Foundation, 2004, pp. 60–61.

Action Assignment #16

Take a trip back in time and recall all the times in your life where you thought you were headed in one direction and then you ended up traveling in another. Try as you might to regain your original footing, you nevertheless were "called" to trod the new path in front of you. How did this change in itinerary turn out? How or why do you think you were directed to travel down a new road?

Read Robert Frost's "The Road Not Taken" below, and consider how your life may have been (or is currently being impacted) in a similar fashion. What are you being called to become?

The Road Not Taken

Two roads diverged in a yellow wood,
And sorry I could not travel both
And be one traveler, long I stood
And looked down one as far as I could
To where it bent in the undergrowth;

Then took the other, as just as fair,
And having perhaps the better claim
Because it was grassy and wanted wear,
Though as for that the passing there
Had worn them really about the same,

And both that morning equally lay
In leaves no step had trodden black.
Oh, I marked the first for another day!
Yet knowing how way leads on to way
I doubted if I should ever come back.

I shall be telling this with a sigh
Somewhere ages and ages hence:
Two roads diverged in a wood, and I,
I took the one less traveled by,
And that has made all the difference.

–Robert Frost

Chapter 17

In reality, it is the sum total of a man's mental attitudes, as well as mental attributes, that makes his life a success or a failure.
– Erna Ferrell Grabe & Paul C. Ferrell

Patterns, when used, bring about predictable outcomes. These outcomes become habitual when we apply them often over time. Soon our actions are set on automatic pilot, and we no longer have to think about the process. We see this in driving a car, reciting memorized prayers, general cooking, and in doing just about anything that we take for granted. Our minds program us for behaviors that are repetitive based on how we performed those behaviors in the past. This can be both the good and the bad news!

The good news is that habits that sustain us and enrich our lives are ones we continue to replicate. The bad news is that habits that are deleterious to us operate exactly the same. So, in preparation for spring cleaning, it might be a good time to look at habit cleansing as a ritual we want to adopt quarterly during the year.

Through lack of persistence, personal initiative, self-discipline, accurate thinking, and controlled attention, a person can become lazy and fall prey to habits that are not conducive to success. These can become at first "a cobweb and then a cable" in their hold upon us. It is always easier to see these negative habits in others, but acknowledging them in ourselves is the first positive step in a new direction.

Being the best "YOU" you can become involves honestly looking at yourself inside and out and making an inventory of your pluses and minuses. An honest appraisal may assist you in determining why your desired goal or outcome remains in the distance. This inventory should not be about judgment, but about improvement. Continuous improvement is what makes the world a better place, not a goal of perfection.

So, tackle a habit you prefer not to have in your repertoire. Is it procrastination? Then force yourself to act. Is it sleeping late? Set the clock for a reasonable time to awaken and don't hit the snooze button. Is it lack of exercise? Pack your gym bag the night before and have it waiting by the door. Whatever it is, you can overcome the undesirable habit by replacing it with a good one.

Spring is time for renewal, and there is no better subject for renewal than yourself!

The R2A2 Formula: How to Recognize, Relate, Assimilate, and Apply Success Principles

by W. Clement Stone & Napoleon Hill

Your ability to recognize, relate, assimilate and use the PMA Principles will give you the power to open any door, meet any challenge, overcome any obstacle and achieve wealth, health, happiness and the true riches of life.

The PMA Science of Success Course is comprised of seventeen fundamental principles that have stood the test of time. They can be compared to an orchestra that is composed of different sections—strings, brass, woodwinds, and percussion—which complement each other and produce a melodious, full, and pleasant sound. Think of yourself as the maestro of your own orchestra of self-help principles. The ability to recognize, relate, assimilate and apply the PMA principles is your baton. Use it to blend all seventeen principles into a symphony of success—a meaningful and productive life.

Like any formula, the R2A2 formula is made up of individual parts. Let's analyze each ingredient.

- ***Re**cognize*: to identify the principle, idea, or technique
- ***Re**late*: to connect or join together; to establish a relationship to your own life

- ***Assimilate***: to make similar or alike: to incorporate; to absorb; to become a part of your thinking and action
- ***Apply***: follow through and act upon

Each ingredient in the formula is important and has special meaning; when combined, they will lead you to success. By using the formula, you will be able to focus the spotlight on the Success Principles that directed and guided Napoleon Hill and many other successful people to achieve their objectives. The same principles will help you achieve your Definite Major Goals in Life.

How To Develop The Habit Of Using The R2 A2 Formula

First of all, you need a mental success reflex, a trigger phrase that will immediately direct your mind when you recognize a success principle, idea or technique.

Example

Recognize: I recognize the principle, idea or technique that is being used. It helped someone else—I can see the results—and it will work for me if I use it. "That's for me!"

Relate: Ask yourself, "What will the success principle, idea or technique do for me? IMPORTANT: You must relate it to yourself. Start with the most important living person as far as you are concerned: YOU.

Assimilate: "How can I use principles, ideas or techniques to achieve my goals or solve my problems? How can I absorb them into my behavior so that they become a part of me? How can I develop a success habit—a success reflex so that the right thing will be done?"

Apply: "What action will I take?" "When am I going to start?" Ask yourself these important questions and then follow through with the self-starter: DO IT NOW! Yes, DO IT NOW!

The R2A2 formula should become so ingrained in your mind that you can recognize success principles, ideas, or techniques by listening to a sermon or an inspirational recording, reading a newspaper or magazine article or a self-help book, and by studying the lives of great men and women. *Remember: Develop and use your own success reflex by seeking ways to say "That's for me!"...*

PMA Science of Success, Educational Edition. The Napoleon Hill Foundation, 1961, pp. x–xi.

Action Assignment #17

In light of "habit cleansing," read Dr. Hill's R2A2 Formula and review each of the 17 Success Principles following the example. Next, design 17 improvements in your personal habit profile, and make the changes!

For example, under Maintenance of Sound Health, go cold turkey and say "No Texting While Driving!" Then, put the phone away until you stop or arrive at your destination. If you continue to live, that will surely assist you in maintaining sound health! A slight improvement in each of the 17 areas will serve you well and each positive addiction will add up to making the very best you that you can become, one positive habit at a time.

Chapter 18

We may not labor at what we dream: but the whistling boy has the willing team, and a little song makes a shorter seam.

– Douglas Malloch

Recently I purchased a young canary and I am trying to coax it to sing. Fortunately in the same room with the cage is a computer with speakers, so in the morning I am able to play multiple canaries singing in the proper fashion. My canary gets excited as he hears the warbling and jumps around his cage from perch to feed cup to swing, but has yet to warble. Today I saw him open his beak as if to orchestrate a new sound, but no new notes came forth!

I watch him tilt his head, listen attentively, and recognize the song he is yet to sing, but I am still waiting. This reminds me of simple steps most people fail to take on the road to success. I often read that success is something that is reserved for the chosen few and cannot be coaxed or practiced or honed to a higher level, but I disagree.

Success, like anything in life, is a skill we acquire through learning, and learning is a process. We crawl before we walk, and we walk before we run. I have never seen or heard of a baby jumping out of a crib in a full run. Likewise, I have never seen or met a true overnight success. Success, became it is an acquired trait, takes practice, practice, and more practice before the desired end result appears for all to see. If it looks easy, I can confirm that it is not. Don't be fooled by appearances.

Just as with my canary, people do not see the practice but love to acclaim the performance. It may appear easy in retrospect. However, through suggestion, conditioning, practice, and more practice, the end result will be that I know why my caged bird sings, and I also know why success is achieved by those who try, and try, and try, and finally succeed!

If you want to achieve success, find those "songs" that you can imitate, and then keep working at the notes until you tune into the true melody that leads to a spectacular performance.

The Effect of Music on Human Behavior

by Napoleon Hill

If the truth were known it might disclose the fact that music has been the strongest factor in producing the geniuses of the past. You do not have to go outside of your own experiences to prove that your most elevating thoughts come to you under the stimulating influence of music.

No man can say what music has played and is now playing in unfolding and giving greater proportions to man's higher aspirations and in separating mankind from the baser animal instincts with which all of us are still too closely linked. No man can say that the musicians have not played a powerful part in bringing civilization up to its present standard.

Of all the people in the world who feel deeply, who pour their very heart and soul into their work, who are bound closely by that golden cord called sympathy for mankind, it seems that the musicians stand at the top of the list.

It is a proved fact that music will calm an angry person in a few seconds' time. No normal person can long withstand the rhythmic vibrations of music without falling into harmony with it and being swept away on its wings, into a feeling of quietness and sereneness.

Napoleon Hill's Magazine. Vol. 1, No. 1 (April, 1921), p. 18.

Action Assignment #18

Napoleon Hill tells us that he believes music has been one of the strongest factors, if not the strongest factor, in producing geniuses of the past. Therefore, I suggest that listening to music may be a way to increase your success performance. But, not just any music. Rather, music that is aligned to the 17 Success Principles works best.

Create a playlist based upon the principles in the order of their appearance and select music that speaks to you and promotes a higher state of consciousness in you! In other words, these selections should elevate you to your higher self. You may also want to begin with an Overture and end with a Finale to complete your masterpiece!

Chapter 19

A graceful behavior towards superiors, inferiors, and equals is a constant source of pleasure. It pleases others because it indicates respect for their personality; but it gives tenfold more pleasure to ourselves.
– Samuel Smiles

Healing professionals come to us in many shapes and sizes. Whether we call them nurses, teachers, or even angels is our discretion. The person who enters into our life at just the right moment, provides us the help, motivation, or inspiration that is needed, and then leaves us with improved health and an enhanced state of mind is truly a godsend. The "teacher" always shows up when the student is ready.

This can work in reverse too. Each of us can become an instrument of change sent to someone in need. Whether we reach out via a chance encounter, through a writing such as this, or in a professional capacity when helping someone in need, a change for good can occur if we allow the force for good to flow through us. As a vehicle or vessel for spirit, we provide the potential for good to survive in the world.

Elisabeth Kübler-Ross wrote about the process of death and dying and documented five stages in the process. If you consider change, it is the same process. Denial, Anger, Bargaining, Depression and Acceptance are the sequential stages. Each one is a step toward a new life whether on the earthly or spiritual plane.

The best service professionals put people first. They care about the people they serve above and beyond the product they deliver. Shakespeare, Emerson, Aristotle, Mother Teresa, and Joan of Arc are all significant teachers from the past but they are only relevant today if they help someone process through their own journey in life. Just as advances in medicine are only useful if they enable doctors and nurses to deliver an improved quality of life for their patients, so too personal gifts are only relevant if they help the recipient in the area where help is needed.

In reality, each and every one of us is put here to serve in some capacity. Our degree of service determines the love we receive from others. This "love" is our spiritual bank account, and far exceeds any financial reward we may accrue in our portfolio of assets and investments. Emphasis needs to be placed on a balance between the two. Love and money do make the world go round, but too much or not enough of one or the other makes a very imbalanced and unstable person.

So, thank a nurse, a teacher, a minister, and your banker, financial advisor, and employer for providing you with the tools to make a better life for yourself and most importantly for the others you deal with on a daily basis. Give and take is the ebb and flow of the universe, but be sure that while you are on the receiving end, you are equally aligned with the giving end.

Positive Mental Attitude

by Napoleon Hill

Whether you write, preach sermons, sell merchandise or service, or produce food from the soil of the earth, you can and you should learn *to be yourself* at all times; and remember always that the one thing people frown upon is a "phony" who tries to imitate others.

Learn to relate yourself to every circumstance which influences your life as something which happened for the best, for it may well be that your saddest experience will bring you your greatest assets if you will give time a chance to mellow the experience.

If you should ever be so unfortunate as to feel the urge for power over others against their will, squelch that desire before it destroys you, and *divert that urge to better control over your own mind.*

Use your mind to shape your destiny to fulfill whatever purposes in life you choose, and to avail yourself of all the riches which come in that sealed envelope labeled Rewards. Keep your mind so busy doing the things you want to do that no time will be left for it to stray into the things you do not want.

PMA Science of Success, Educational Edition. Napoleon Hill Foundation, 1961, p. 227.

Action Assignment #19

Review the five stages of Death and Dying identified by Elisabeth Kübler-Ross in her first book, *On Death and Dying,* published in 1969. They are: Denial (this isn't happening to me!), Anger (why is this happening to me?), Bargaining (I promise I'll be a better person *if*...), Depression (I don't care anymore), and Acceptance (I'm ready for whatever comes).

Now, consider three significant changes that have occurred in your life. Going through the five steps, detail your experience with each of the stages. Use the prompts to jumpstart your memory. Notice that each time when you reached the Acceptance Stage you were ready to move beyond past experiences and grow beyond where you were before. This cycle of change can be identified in all lives. As we work through the cycle we grow beyond where we initially found ourselves. When you accept your past experiences and learn from them, you can next begin to create a better future.

Chapter 20

Do you wish the world were happy? Then remember day by day, just to scatter seeds of kindness as you pass along the way,
– Ella Wheeler Wilcox

A common thread throughout humanity is mothers. May is traditionally the month to honor mothers in the Western World. Days warm, flowers bloom, eggs hatch, and the air is filled with wonderful scents from the season of rebirth and renewal. In Greek mythology this was the time when Demeter's daughter Persephone returned from the underworld and in Demeter's rejoicing the landscape blossomed. Also, the Biblical passage "Behold, I make all things new," is displayed for all to see in our yards and gardens. This reminds us that Earth is our mother too. Emerson states "the Earth laughs in flowers," and we can see this just by observing springtime. Enjoying our natural surroundings is a good way to invoke happiness and a Positive Mental Attitude.

In gratitude, we are thankful, the earth is thankful, and our spirits lift. Napoleon Hill reminds us that in Going the Extra Mile we are placing the Universe in our debt. What a wonderful way to describe the good Karma that can be earned simply by doing the right thing. It does not take a hero or a heroine to do the right thing. It just takes movement towards the good and away from the bad. As we move in the right direction, all things begin to change for the good one small step at a time.

Why not honor all mothers this month by doing the right thing? Pick up litter, clean a space, plant some flowers, sweep your doorstep, wash a pet, clear clutter, and begin to give things a new lease on life. Take the time and make the time to do your part in the rebirth and renewal of our small home space and in our larger home—Planet

Earth—as well. As Gandhi so aptly states: Be the change you wish to see in the world.

The Hand That Rocks the Cradle

by Napoleon Hill

This month we dedicate this page to the tired little woman who cares for the children, mends their clothes, washes their faces, teaches them their prayers and eats at the last table. There is one of these women in nearly every home, but her name is seldom mentioned in the society columns and never in "Who's Who," yet it is to her love and patience and inspiration that men owe that which they proudly refer to as their own achievements in life. In the mad rush for glory and fame and dollars let us not forget the hand that rocks the cradle. We may not raise ourselves in the estimate of men, by honoring her as she is entitled to be honored, but, by doing so we are not apt to lower ourselves in the eyes of God.

Napoleon Hill's Magazine. Volume I, Number 6 (October, 1921), Back Cover.

Action Assignment #20

Dr. Napoleon Hill reaches across time to give you this week's action assignment himself. As he mentally taps you on the shoulder, remember to stay the course. Dr. Hill states:

> You are constantly building your character out of the impressions you gather from your daily environment, therefore you can shape your character as you wish. If you would build it strongly, surround yourself with the pictures of the great men and women you most admire; hang mottoes of positive affirmation on the walls of your room; place the books of your favorite authors on

the table where you can get at them often, and read those books with pencil in hand, marking the lines which bring you the noblest thoughts; fill your mind with the biggest and noblest and most elevating thoughts, and soon you will begin to see your own character taking on the hue and color of this environment which you have created for yourself.

Napoleon Hill's Magazine. Volume I, Number 10 (March, 1922), Back Cover.

CHAPTER 21

The whole course of things goes to teach us faith. We need only obey. There is guidance for each of us, and by lowly listening we shall hear the right word.

– Ralph Waldo Emerson

At a thrift shop this weekend I picked up a book on angels for a friend whose passion is angels. It is an interesting book because it was designed as a fundraising tool for a not-for-profit organization. The person who compiled the book came up with the idea of asking celebrities to describe their personal angel in either written or artistic format. Some individuals shared a drawing, some shared a short description, and some shared brief stories about angelic encounters they had in their own lives. As I leafed through the book, I found the illustrations and commentaries uplifting to view and to read, and I also felt inspired to ask myself the question as to whether or not I believe in angels and how or when I may have encountered them in my life.

In the referenced book the author indicates that angels often take on ordinary appearances and we may not recognize them at first sight. It is only later, in retrospect, that we may realize we have been guided from above and received a divine intervention or spiritual helping hand. We must have eyes to see and to appreciate that which is around us before these things can have significance for our inner selves. Beauty can be seen and ignored, or appreciated for the miracle it is depending upon the insight of the person doing the viewing.

Napoleon Hill talks a great deal about the receptivity that must be present for an idea to blossom within ourselves. He states that when we are inspired, we need to act immediately on the inspiration and not question it. Ideas that are not acted upon are stillborn ideas. They are never "birthed" into reality, and are therefore merely wishes that amount to nothing. Some people are said to be so lazy that they are too lazy to even wish for the good things of life, but want others to do the wishing for them! Dr. Hill states: "If wishes were horses, beggars would ride."

Angels might be likened to inspirations that have landed in our thoughts and spread their wings to become full blown ideas that are then delivered into our world. When you see a thing in its fullness beyond merely looking at it, you are gazing upon an angel. I like to think that higher thoughts are angelic presences that raise the bar for human performance. When we receive these thoughts, it is the acting upon them that makes all the difference. If we hesitate, reconsider, fail to respond, or simply are too lazy to take up the cause at hand, then we have declined the opportunity a "thoughtful" angel has given to us.

What seeds of greatness has your angel sown into the field of your imagination today? Which ones will you cultivate?

Catch the Spirit

by Napoleon Hill

We who desire to accumulate riches, should remember the real leaders of the world always have been men who harnessed, and put into practical use, the intangible, unseen forces of unborn opportunity, and have converted those forces, (or impulses of thought), into sky-scrapers, cities, factories, airplanes, automobiles, and every form of convenience that makes life more pleasant.

Tolerance, and an open mind are practical necessities of the dreamer of today. Those who are afraid of new ideas are doomed before they start. Never has there been a time more favorable to pioneers than the present. True, there is no wild and woolly west to be conquered, as in the days of the Covered Wagon: but there is a vast business, financial, and industrial world to be remoulded and redirected along new and better lines.

In planning to acquire your share of the riches, let no one influence you to scorn the dreamer. To win the big stakes in this changed world, you must catch the spirit of the great pioneers of the past, whose dreams have given to civilization all that it has of value, the spirit which serves as the life-blood of our own country—your opportunity and mine, to develop and market our talents.

Think and Grow Rich. The Ralston Society, 1937, pp 45–46.

Action Assignment #21

Consider whether or not you have had any experiences of divine intervention in your own life.

We know for a fact that if one person can experience something, we all can because our human DNA is so strikingly similar that there is only an infinitesimal difference in one human from another. If one is capable, we are all capable. Just as in body-building, activities contribute to our advancement. So too in spirit-building, activities in this realm heighten our awareness and advancement.

Today, be open to the gifts of the spirit. Listen to the still small voice within, and respond to the prompt to do as requested. When that nudge comes your way, as Dr. Hill states, act on it. Do not hesitate. Next, list the ways you have been inspired this week in your journal. Then, most importantly, indicate which inspirations you accepted and brought into your conscious world? These are the ones that will make a true difference in your life and the lives of others. These are your angelic gifts.

CHAPTER 22

Just take off your coat and go to it; just start to sing as you tackle the thing that "couldn't be done," and you'll do it.

– Edgar Guest

Discipline is something that every one of us needs, but few of us want. The most beneficial type of discipline is self-discipline, and the reason is that if we can effectively discipline ourselves then we do not have to be disciplined by others. This makes us more effective as leaders because the initiative for positive action is within us. No one has to coax, cajole, beg, nag, or trick us into behaving at our best. Innately, we know the process and what results it delivers. A self-disciplined person constantly decides to be his very best via one self-determined act at a time.

Early in life parents begin by disciplining their children in order to help them develop correct patterns of behavior for the society in which they live. Children follow along but also witness their parents' behaviors. This is where most behaviors and values are "caught" and not "taught." In order to emulate Mom and Dad, their first and most important teachers, children model the behaviors that they see being performed. That is why children seldom do as they are told, but mimic what they see. If parents want good, replicable results, then they must be the role models they want for their children. It does little good to remind a child to keep their room clean, if the parents do not embrace the same goal.

As adults, when we discipline ourselves our life goes better. The Laws of the Universe are predictable and observable. Our best results occur when we work in tandem with these rules rather than rebel against them. As we emulate the way nature works we begin to fit ourselves into the divine scheme of things. It is said, as without so within. Our lives are the result of the choices that we make. By taking command of our self and sacrificing the pleasure of immediate gratification, we can begin to delay gratification and reach higher, more ideal levels of performance. Why settle for a burger on Monday night, when through delayed gratification and the saving habit you can have that steak you really wanted all along on Saturday? Learn to first save a little to earn a lot!

Self-Discipline

by Napoleon Hill

No other single requirement for individual success is as important as self-discipline. Self-discipline, or self-control, means taking possession of your own mind.... All of the principles of this philosophy are for the express purpose of enabling you to develop control over yourself. The matter of self-discipline is one of the greatest of all essentials for success. Indeed, if one cannot master himself, he has little hope of mastering anything or anyone else....

Self-discipline begins with the mastery of your thoughts. If you do not control your thoughts, you cannot control your deeds. Therefore, in its simplest form, self-discipline causes you to think first and act afterward. Almost everyone automatically does exactly the reverse of this. People generally act first and think later—unless they take possession of their minds and control their thoughts and deeds through self-discipline.

PMA Science of Success, Educational Edition. Napoleon Hill Foundation, 1961, pp. 267–268.

Action Assignment #22

Invite the good things into your life through delayed gratification.

Instead of buying on impulse, select one fine (perhaps even overpriced) item that you would simply love to have. Invest in purchasing that item via a small change "jar" savings account located on your dresser. At night deposit only your loose change that has accumulated throughout the day. With the goal being the price of the item you want on the lid of the change jar, count your contributions once a week and work toward the purchase price of the item until you have achieved it.

When you arrive at your goal, treat yourself to that special purchase and enjoy your delayed gratification.

Chapter 23

The secret of a better and more successful life is to cast out those old dead, unhealthy thoughts. Substitute for them new vital, dynamic faith thoughts. You can depend upon it—an inflow of new thoughts will remake you and your life.

– *Norman Vincent Peale*

Isn't anticipation a wonderful thing in life? When looking forward to something in the future we create new interests in our present moment in time. Rather than being nostalgic about the past, we can anticipate the future and the joys that it will bring. The events do not have to be large, grandiose events. Even small events will do to put us in forward focus. Daily I look outside on my cobblestone patio to see if my peonies have bloomed. Today, no peonies were showing off yet, but I will still check on them tomorrow. However, where one white bearded iris stood tall and majestic yesterday in my nearby flower garden today over seven had bloomed to create a tour de force. I always enjoy the surprising, unexpected gifts that nature delivers to our doorstep.

Anticipate birthdays, vacations, movies, dinners, walks in the park, lunches with friends, a phone call from a loved one, a dog or cat coming to greet you by the front door, a special "hello" from a long ago friend, a card in the mail, a "happy" gram, and many, many other standard events, all contribute to a more positive mental attitude. Too often we become accustomed to immediate gratification, and like the memory of food too hastily eaten the pleasure is diminished because of the hurried way we rush through the event. Immediately, we rush on to the next "thing" and miss the essence of the "thing" that just transpired in our lives. Maybe we were preoccupied with out cell phone or our internet connection. The only connection worth maintaining is our human connection, and that can be easily displaced if we confuse technology with living a purposeful life.

Today, anticipate the things that you would miss most if no longer available to you. The voice of a loved one, the smell of brewing coffee in the morning, the chirp of a canary awakening to a new day, the purr of a cat, the taste of raspberries, the comfort of friendship, the phone call just to say "hello" and that you are missed, and on and on. As your day wears on, think about this things that give you power in the moment, and express true gratitude for them with the anticipation that they will be with you for many years to come. As you anticipate, so too you create, because what you think about you bring about. May you bring about all the goodness and richness that life has to offer one positive outcome at a time.

Source of Power

by Napoleon Hill

You will observe that neither success nor failure is the result of luck or chance. I warn you, before you read further, that the knowledge you are about to receive will forever deprive you of the privilege of resorting to alibis to explain away your failures. I warn you, too, that you will never again be privileged to say truthfully that life never gave you an opportunity, for you will know definitely that as long as you have the right to form and express your own thoughts you have the potential power with which to change the circumstances of your life to whatever you wish them to be.

If your life is not what you wish it to be, you can truthfully say that you drifted into your present unhappy condition through the irresistible force of Cosmic Habit-force, but you cannot stop there because you shall know presently that time and Definiteness of Purpose, backed by Cosmic Habit-force, can give you rebirth no matter who you are or what may be your circumstances.

You may be in prison, without friends or money, with a life sentence hanging over you, but you can walk through the front gate and back to the outside world a free man, if you adapt yourself to this force in the proper manner. How do I know this can be done? Because it has been done before. Because your common sense will tell you that it can be done once you understand the working principle and catch the full significance of its relationship to time and Definiteness of Purpose.

You are going to make another outstanding discovery in connection with this force. You are going to learn that "every failure brings with it the seed of an equivalent advantage." You are going to discover, beyond any room for doubt, that every experience, every circumstance of your life is a potential stepping stone or a stumbling block, due entirely to the manner in which you react to the circumstance in your own mind.

The Wisdom of Andrew Carnegie. The Napoleon Hill Foundation, 2004, pp. 290–291.

Action Assignment #23

Turn your face toward the good and away from the bad.

When a person asks, "How are you?" isn't the usual response a litany of ills and misfortunes rather than the gifts the Universe delivers? Details can be given in length about anything and everything that has gone wrong, rather than what has gone right.

Beginning with only one hour each day for a week, concentrate only on the goodness that life has to offer. Be a good-finder rather than a fault-finder. Locate and record the good that you uncover because you consciously decide to focus on the good. Is your grass too high? Focus instead on the abundant rainfall that made the grass grow tall and green.

Is your mailbox in need of repair? Focus instead on it serving as a vehicle for mail received at home without the necessity of driving to a post office. Is your car in need of detailing? Focus instead on the fact that you have reliable transportation at the turn of a key.

Now, it's your turn. For an hour each day turn the tables and focus on the goodness—the seed of an equivalent or greater benefit—inside each annoyance or adversity that you encounter. Therein you will find the rewards of a life well lived.

Chapter 24

A person lives effectively when he uses his powers to the full; and to use his powers to the full he needs a well-adjusted, smooth-running machinery of living.

– James L. Mursell

When we do the same things it is not uncommon to expect the same results. This works well if we are satisfied with the results that we are receiving, but does not work well if we find ourselves stuck, depressed, and feeling left on the sidelines of life. Perhaps by exploring new things that are somewhat extraneous to our current lifestyles we can open up new avenues of enrichment that will make our lives more enjoyable and productive.

The world is said to be our oyster, but we are not guaranteed the pearl unless we do the work to find it. Too often individuals who find life less than enjoyable have failed to fan the flame of new experiences. What is there new to do you might ask? The list is literally endless. Take a course, read a book, watch a new channel, adjust your daily schedule, visit a nearby town that you have not explored before as if you were a tourist, take the day off as a mental health day and drive in the opposite direction that you normally go, eat at an ethnic restaurant, visit a healing center, attend a different denomination of church than you belong to, rent a car or truck that you have not driven before, and begin today to enrich your life through action. Dr. Seuss says it best:

Oh, the Places You'll Go!

Congratulations!
Today is your day.

You're off to Great Places!
You're off and away!

You have brains in your head.
You have feet in your shoes
You can steer yourself
any direction you choose.
You're on your own.
And you know what you know.
And YOU are the guy who'll decide where to go.

– Theodor Geisel, aka Dr. Seuss

Now, take up the challenge and decide what new opportunities you will create for yourself.

The Foundation of Habits

by Napoleon Hill

Cosmic habitforce, acting through the subconscious mind, picks up one's mental attitude and translates it into the material equivalent, by employing normal natural laws and principles, and primarily by inspiring the man himself with a plan by which he may accomplish his purposes.

Cosmic habitforce is always and everywhere at work, translating one's mental attitude into its material equivalent. One does not have to worry about the working of the law: it works automatically. To gain the benefits of the law, one has only to take possession of his own mind, by making it predominately positive through his daily thought habits, and planting in it a definite picture of his desires.

The principle by which an idea germinates and grows and becomes a habit has been designated as cosmic habitforce. It may be called any other name, so long as you recognize the power. Its working principle is definite; it has been used and demonstrated by

the greatest men in the world. And it never fails. It works as well on behalf of the humble person as for the business magnate. Its purpose is to perpetuate everything after its own kind, including the thought habits of man, and to maintain a balanced status quo in the universe, under the direction of Infinite Intelligence.

PMA Science of Success, Educational Edition. Napoleon Hill Foundation, 1961, pp. 513–514.

Action Assignment #24

Begin today to create your own bucket list of things you want to do before you can't.

Challenge yourself to come up with a minimum of 100 items and number them 1 through 100 in no special order. Give yourself a 3–5 year time frame, and then begin to scratch the items off your list as you do them. Better yet, take a photo of yourself doing the activity and make a 100-picture photo collage of yourself accomplishing these very things. Instead of "I can't do ..." state "I am doing ..." and empower yourself.

Yesterday, I shared a future trip, that might happen a year from now, with someone and asked the person if they would consider going. The response was, "I probably can't afford it!" This response came before any price was either investigated or quoted. My question is,"How do you know you can't, or is it really you WON'T?" Open up new horizons for yourself by first saying "YES!" and then figuring out how it CAN be done.

Chapter 25

Continually affirming establishes the belief in the subconscious. It would not be necessary to make an affirmation more than once if one had perfect faith! One should not plead or supplicate, but give thanks repeatedly, that he has received.

– Florence Scovel Shinn

How are you at Napoleon Hill trivia? Take this quick quiz and perhaps learn something new or at least acquire some "ice breakers" for your social next event. Answers at the bottom. No peeking!

1. What year was Napoleon Hill commissioned by Andrew Carnegie?
2. When was *Law of Success* published?
3. What was Napoleon Hill's first name?
4. Napoleon Hill's father attended a correspondence school after he married Martha Ramey Banner in order to become a licensed _____?
5. What year was *Think and Grow Rich* published?
6. At what type of event did Napoleon Hill first meet W. Clement Stone?
7. Sexual transmutation is simply the exchange of one type of _____ for another.
8. Napoleon Hill's Imaginary Counselors were individuals in real life that Hill _____.
9. The Eight Guiding Princes were assigned to watch over Dr. Hill's Financial Prosperity, Sound Health, Peace of Mind, Hope, Faith, Love, Romance, and _____?

10. Dr. Hill often refers to our other self as our _____.
11. The seven basic fears include: fear of poverty, criticism, ill health, loss of love, loss of liberty, old age, and _____?
12. Napoleon Hill's famous quotation states: "What the mind can conceive and believe, the mind can _____."
13. The 17 Success Principles are: Definiteness of Purpose, Mastermind Alliance, _____, Going the Extra Mile, _____, Personal Initiative, Positive Mental Attitude, _____, Self-Discipline, Accurate Thinking, Controlled Attention, _____, Learning from Adversity and Defeat, Creative Vision, Maintenance of Sound Health, Budgeting Time and Money, and _____.
14. Napoleon Hill was born on _____.
15. Napoleon Hill died on _____.
16. Napoleon Hill is buried at _____.
17. Napoleon Hill's son Blair was born without _____.
18. According to Napoleon Hill, no one ever does anything without a _____, or _____.
19. Napoleon Hill states that: "When you give directives to your subconscious mind, be definite and clearly state your desires, and you will not be disappointed, provided you _____your directives with strong BELIEF that they will be carried out."
20. Napoleon Hill states that _____ is the comptroller of the Universe.

How did you do?

Follow These Orders

by Napoleon Hill

Since the subconscious translates into their logical conclusion all thoughts which reach it—whether they are good or bad for the individual—it is clearly suggested that the way to put the subconscious mind to work for one in a helpful way is by giving it definite orders as to what is desired.

When it comes to giving orders to the subconscious mind, there are some instructions which must be carried out to the letter:

a. Write out a clear statement of that which you wish your subconscious mind to act upon, and set a definite time within which you wish action. Memorize this statement and repeat it to yourself, orally, hundreds of times daily, especially just before going to sleep.
b. When you repeat your statement BELIEVE that it will be acted upon by your subconscious mind, and see yourself already in possession of that which your statement calls for. Close your statement by expressing gratitude for having received what you asked for.
c. Before repeating your statement to your subconscious, work yourself into a high, intense state of emotional enthusiasm and joy because of your inner feeling that your request will be fulfilled. The subconscious acts almost instantaneously on thoughts which are expressed in any state of high emotion, either negative or positive. This last statement is highly significant. Please read it again and think about it.

You Can Work Your Own Miracles. Ballantine, 1996, pp. 138–139.

Action Assignment #25

A good device for instilling positive thought and affirmations in your subconscious mind is the memorization of quotations.

Since we are learning about Napoleon Hill's famous works, why not select 10–20 meaningful quotations that assist you in achieving your definite major purpose and commit them to memory? When you need them the most, they will pop up in your mental awareness just like toast pops up in a toaster, and you can then condition yourself for the success that will be delivered to you right on schedule.

Napoleon Hill states: "The subconscious mind will not act upon any idea, plan, or purpose which is not clearly expressed to it." Therefore, doesn't it make sense to feed the subconscious mind good thoughts that it needs to activate a positive mental attitude?

Begin with the quotation, "What the mind can conceive and believe, the mind can achieve." Now, add 19 more and commit them to memory until they become rote. As the need arises, these thoughts will race to your aid and assist you in the maintenance of a positive mental attitude.

Trivia Answers:

1. 1908
2. 1928
3. Oliver
4. Dentist
5. 1937
6. Chicago Luncheon
7. Energy
8. Admired
9. Wisdom
10. Higher Self
11. Death
12. Achieve
13. Applied Faith, Pleasing Personality, Enthusiasm, Teamwork, Cosmic Habitforce
14. October 26, 1883
15. November 8, 1970
16. Frederick Memorial Gardens, Gaffney, South Carolina
17. Ears
18. Motive, Motives
19. Emotionalize
20. Cosmic Habitforce

Chapter 26

Greatness is not measured in any material terms. It is not measured in inches, dollars, acres, votes, hurrahs, or by any other of the world's yardsticks or barometers. Greatness is measured in spiritual terms. It is education. It is life expansion.

– *Ralph Parlette*

Being a true companion to someone, whether in a conversation or in a relationship, requires a thorough and honest exchange of information. Simply talking about the weather and what you ate for lunch does not qualify unless you are a meteorologist, a nutritionist or a chef. Too often the people in life we are closest to in proximity know the least about us. On the other hand, strangers who we meet by the wayside in life may be the ones that we patch into our secret selves. Why is it that for those closest we never ignite the spark and share a meaningful conversation?

Who we are is determined by our dreams and our desires that are really the blueprint of our souls. If we are to become the architect of our lives, we also need a general contractor who takes the blueprint and actualizes it into where our dreams take us. If truth be known we are both the architect and the contractor and the carpenter and the maintenance man and all else, because we are the mechanism that controls our outcome in life. If we merely discuss it in a superficial way in passing, this generality will cause us to arrive at whatever destination the Universe throws at us—not the destination that we dreamed about and desired for ourselves.

What is your heart's desire? Have you verbalized it? Written it down? Shared it with the person closest to you? Or will you let it wither and die on the vine? The choice, obviously, is yours and yours alone. If you just want to live an existence in the median of life, then your rewards will be mediocre. If you walk on the perimeters and look for the unusual and awaken interests that will fulfill your heart's desire, then truly you will be amazed at the richness and wholeness life has to offer. So, where will you place your next footstep? I hope it detours from the traditional path that the majority of humanity walks. Detour, and take that one small step that will enable you to arrive at new and uncharted shores.

Habits of Growth

by Napoleon Hill

The whole purpose of education, or so it should be at least, is to start the mind of the individual to growing and developing *from within;* to cause the mind to evolve and expand through constant changes in the thinking processes, so that the individual may eventually become acquainted with his own potential powers and thereby be capable of solving his personal problems.

Evidence that this theory conforms with nature's plans may be found in the fact that the better educated people of all times are those who graduate from the great UNIVERSITY OF HARD KNOCKS, through experiences *which force them to develop and use their mind-power.*

The law of change is one of the greatest of all sources of education! Understand this truth and you will no longer oppose the changes which give you a wider scope of understanding of yourself and the world at large. And you will no longer resist nature's breaking up of some of the habits you have formed *which have not brought you peace of mind or material riches.*

The traits the Creator most emphatically frowns upon in human beings are complacency, self-satisfaction, procrastination, fear and self-imposed limitations, all of which carry heavy penalties which are exacted from those who indulge such traits.

Through the law of change, man is forced to keep on growing. Whenever a nation, a business institution, or an individual, ceases to change and settles into a rut of routine habits, some mysterious power enters and smashes the setup, breaks up the old habits, lays the foundation for new and better habits.

In everything and everyone the law of growth is through eternal change!

You Can Work Your Own Miracles. Ballantine, 1996, pp. 29–30.

Action Assignment #26

This issue marks the half-way point in our calendar year. To date there have been twenty-five action assignments that you have worked on to increase your self-awareness, personal effectiveness, and leadership skills that are designed to enable you to take immediate action for the advancement and achievement of your personal goals.

Assignment 26 asks you to consider your progress to date. Have you walked on the wild, creative side and opened up new horizons for yourself, or are you still treading your usual path?

View your life as a highway that enables you to arrive at a chosen destination. What course have you charted for yourself? What itinerary are you following? What signposts along the way indicate that you are on course or point you in your chosen direction? How are you calculating the distance? The mileage? The destination? All these things have to be considered just as if you were taking a real journey this week. You would not embark without knowing where you are going or when you are to arrive. So too, you need to create a plan and then work the plan to get you to your destination of choice. Are you traveling on a supersonic jumbo jet or still using training wheels? As you can imagine, your altitude is determined by your planning and execution. Get busy and decide to travel first class.

Chapter 27

A good attitude to take is the one you assume when you drop a letter into the mail box. You do not expect to find an answer upon your return to your home. No—you simply drop the letter into the slot and know without specific thinking—that through a chain of events—in due time a reply will reach you.

– Ben Sweetland

Recently I have been thinking about the word *support.* Since I have been in the need of some financial advice, I reflected on the fact that Napoleon Hill directs one to seek the advice of experts in their field who have accumulated the specialized knowledge in your area of need. Therefore, I took my question to my personal banker as he terms himself, and sought his advice. Not only did he spend over 1.5 hours with me, but first he listened closely and attentively to me and then proceeded to point things out things that I had not considered. Next, he directed me to resources that I would not have known about through my own experience. By the time we were finished with the meeting, we had created an action plan that we felt comfortable with for reasons I did not know about prior to the meeting. I felt that I had been granted a gift much like a download of information that prepared me for what I wanted to do next.

I forgot to mention that this person is thirty years old and I am 63, but I forfeited the differential in age between us to gain the knowledge that he has. I could have rationalized that I needed a more mature person to talk to, but I have confidence in this person and he was there to offer his guidance and support. There is that word again—support. All of us can offer it just by showing up and sharing the information that we have that can in turn be beneficial to others. This is huge for the person who needs the help, and cost free to the person who is giving it.

But, this generosity is often not offered. People may feel that it is a brain drain, or will shrink their wisdom capacity or potential as if others were siphoning it off as you would gas from a can. But, that is inaccurate. Each of us has something to give that can be utilized by another. It may be guidance, financial assistance, or even just an open ear into which someone can pour out their heart. Listening can be a cost free alternative that generates goodwill, compassion, useful ideas, and free counseling for those that may need it at the moment. Why withhold this precious gift of guidance?

Be a benefit to someone rather than a hindrance. There is more than enough to go around, and generosity creates abundance in your life and in the lives of others you serve. I'd rather be a go-giver than a go-getter. In striving for more and more personally it seems that people share less and less. Emerson wisely states: "Put God in your debt. Every stroke shall be repaid. The longer the payment is withholden, the better for you; for compound interest on compound interest is the rate and usage of this exchequer."

Now, I ask you, what more could you ask from someone than the opportunity to put God in your debt? That has to be the ultimate jackpot!

Pot of Gold

by Napoleon Hill

Here is the appropriate place to remind you of an important thing about the habit of going the extra mile by doing more than one is paid for. It is the strange influence which it has on the man who does it. The greatest benefit from this habit does not come to those to whom the service is rendered. It comes to the one who renders the service, in the form of a changed "mental attitude," which gives him more influence with other people, more self-reliance, greater initiative, more enthusiasm, more vision and definiteness of purpose. All of these are qualities of successful achievement.

"Do the thing and you shall have the power," said Emerson. Ah, yes the power! What can a man do in our world without power? But it must be the type of power which attracts other people instead of repelling them. It must be a form of power which gains momentum from the law of increasing returns, through the operation of which one's acts and deeds come back to him greatly multiplied.

You who work for wages should learn more about this sowing and reaping business. Then you would understand why no man can go on forever sowing the seed of inadequate service and reaping a harvest of full grown pay. You would know that there must come a halt to the habit of demanding a full day's pay for a poor day's work.

And you who do not work for wages, but who wish to get more of the better things of life! Let us have a word with you. Why do you not become wise and start getting what you wish the easy and sure way? Yes, there is an easy and a sure way to promote one's self into whatever he wants from life, and its secret becomes known to every person who makes it his business to go the extra mile. The secret can be uncovered in no other manner, for it is wrapped up in that extra mile.

The pot of gold at the "end of the rainbow" is not a mere fairy tale! The end of that extra mile is the spot where the rainbow ends, and that is where the pot of gold is hidden.

Few people ever catch up with the "end of the rainbow." When one gets to where he thought the rainbow ended he finds it is still far in the distance. The trouble with most of us is that we do not know how to follow rainbows. Those who know the secret know that the end of the rainbow can be reached only by going the extra mile.

Master Key to Riches. Napoleon Hill Foundation, 1945, revised 1965 by Napoleon Hill.

Action Assignment #27

Find a need and fill it.

Put God in your debt as Ralph Waldo Emerson suggests. Give someone a boost when most needed. It need not be financial. It might be inspirational, spiritual, physical, emotional, social, or mental. Think how you can provide assistance in each of the above categories by sharing what has worked for you in the past with someone. Then listen to those around you and see if you can uplift them by offering gems of wisdom in an area of your personal expertise. Be of service — live to give. Do not live to get. I guarantee that you and the world you serve will be the far better for it. And, truly God is good on His word. He will repay one hundredfold just when you need that download of assistance the most. And, it is 100% secure giving.

Chapter 28

Time is one of the most important ingredients in any successful formula for any human activity. Save time. Invest it wisely.
– W. Clement Stone

How busy are you? Are you too busy to enjoy life? Are you living in the past or the future and not present in the moment? If you answered yes to any or all of these questions, then you can rest assured that you are living a 21st Century lifestyle. As a consequence, most people are a hostage of time these days.

We say that we "spend time," yet we can't purchase it for any amount of money. It is not a commodity, but rather something hard to define and even harder to keep. As Einstein stated, time is relative, and each of us knows this to be true. Hours can stretch to days, and days can evaporate into minutes depending upon our outlook and state of mind. Years can pass quickly, but days drag on. No one can capture exact clock time for us since no one possesses our unique experiences. The truth is that we live moment to moment, and each of these moments is uniquely our own. How we spend these moments is determined by our perception of our worth as individuals.

If we shortchange ourselves, we possess little self-confidence. If we save our moments for a perfect day, that perfect day may never come to pass and we will have banked thousands of moments and literally kept them in limbo waiting for something better to come along. Isn't it time to withdraw some time from your account and spend it on something enjoyable? Now is the time, because now is all we have.

Yesterday, I looked up an old acquaintance on the internet hoping to reconnect with her soon. Well, I hope we don't reconnect as soon as I would have liked because I found out from her obituary that she had passed away a year and a half ago. Again, delays can be points of no return for everyone. In my situation, I had lost the time that I had banked waiting because my friend is no longer here. A missed investment in friendship was lost due to delayed investment. Experience is our best teacher, and the lesson learned is that I will not let this happen again. I will maintain contact with those I consider close because they may not be around when I decide to stay in touch at a later date.

Just for today why not sit and be still and witness time. Time is the greatest gift that we can give anyone because it is priceless. When we share our time with someone and become truly present, we can live outside of time and seemingly pause time for a moment. The sunny afternoon on the beach listening to the waves, the fall foliage drive with smells and colors comingled, the rainy day spent indoors cat napping, and the unending dark night where we wait expectantly for dawn are all opportunities to suspend time and keep a sense of the immortality of the moment in our timeless memories. As we remove ourselves from the daily grind of time, and live in the moment, our perception of time changes and so do we.

Be Particular!

by Napoleon Hill

Analyze your relationships with others and you may be astonished by the amount of time you waste in association with people who cannot possibly be of any value to you; drifters who are going nowhere and are taking plenty of time to get there. Life for many people is just one continuous state of turmoil, friction, confusion and antagonism in human relationships, despite the fact that harmony is one of the fundamental laws of nature without which the whole universe would end in chaos.

It is little wonder, therefore, that many people meet with failure throughout their lives, if we stop to consider that nature forces human beings to absorb and become a part of their daily environments. The most important part of any man's environment is his association with other people. If this association is not one of harmony, the inevitable result is failure.

Successful men choose their daily associates as carefully as they choose their food, and they make sure that their environment is harmonious and thus constructive and beneficial to themselves and to others as well. And they spend no time in the company of people who do not contribute something to their welfare!

"Selfish!" some will exclaim. No, not necessarily selfish. Particular would be the better word.

Successful men know that their lives are influenced by those with whom they associate most intimately, and they so arrange their human relationships that they are influenced in a beneficial way.

PMA Science of Success, Educational Edition. Napoleon Hill Foundation, 1961, pp. 465–466.

Action Assignment #28

Take time today to do something that you consider "out of the ordinary" yet enjoyable.

It is something that you would do, if you only had the time. You do have the time, so do whatever it is that you delay doing because you don't want to waste, spend, or reallocate the time to do it. Ask yourself how many seasons of the year you have left? What is it that as a child you enjoyed doing especially in each season? Was it watching fireworks and smelling the aroma? Was it sitting in the dark outdoors and catching fireflies while star gazing. Was it soaring on a swing and sailing into the air with hands firmly on the ropes as you rose higher and higher? What exactly was it? Now that you have prodded your memory, go out and do just that for fifteen to thirty minutes today. You will find out exactly what "being in the flow" of timelessness means, and you will suspend clock time and truly live and breathe in this absolutely precious moment—your moment in time. Enjoy.

CHAPTER 29

Everything you want or need is trying to happen to you—and it will begin happening to you the moment you learn to say "yes!" to things and conditions that have not yet become reality.

– Jack Boland

Do you have big goals in life? Do these goals ever make you feel selfish or less than entitled? If they do, you are not alone. From childhood we have been cautioned not to be selfish, to freely share, and not get "too big for our britches!" This type of conditioning has seeped into our subconscious programming at a very early age, and causes us undue concern when it rears its ugly head and cautions us to not want too much. This creates a dilemma for us because what our conscious mind attempts to carry out in our waking world is derailed by our subconscious mind as soon as we let down our conscious awareness. Seems like we become our own worst enemy and unfortunately this is true.

Much like a hard drive on our computer, we arrive in adulthood with basic programs that are difficult to override. We may want one thing, but get another. We may exert our very best effort, but find that we never fulfill our highest expectations. We want a successful life, yet continually never make it to the finish line. Now that we know what reins us in, what can we do to replace the programs that our parents, our culture, our teachers, our peers, our systems of belief, and all other societal influences have bequeathed to us? If we knew how to surmount that concern, we would be wealthy beyond measure. More than likely, the problem is universal. However, we can mentally return to the beginning of the installation of our old software, and slowly and systematically begin to replace ineffective programs.

In order to update our existing programs new ones are needed. By consciously giving messages to our subconscious mind especially in the time right before sleep and immediately upon awakening in the morning we can begin to override our programs and better channel our efforts towards success. Simply begin at the beginning by positively affirming that life is good, the universe always works towards our best end result, and day by day we grow better and better.

Sounds too good to be true? Well, it isn't. Life changes because we do and it all begins with a seed of thought. Your thoughts. Your positive thoughts that find fulfillment through positive actions. First assemble the correct internal ingredients and the external will show up in due time.

Neglected Victory Gardens

by Napoleon Hill

The conscious mind is the guardian of the garden spot of the subconscious mind. Neither negative nor positive thoughts can enter the subconscious mind without full consent of the conscious mind except thought *out of the blue*, received through the *sixth sense*. All sense impressions received through the five senses are stopped at the gate by the conscious, thinking mind, for inspection and acceptance or rejection. The conscious mind is therefore a sentry posted to guard the approach to the precious subconscious.

Weeds will grow in abundance in the fertile garden spot of the subconscious if the seeds of preferred crops are not sown. Through *self-suggestion*, you can voluntarily feed your subconscious mind on thoughts of a creative nature or, by neglect, permit thoughts of a destructive nature to find their way into this rich garden.

Definiteness of purpose will keep your mind clear of the things you don't want and keep it so busy working on the things you do want that it will have no time to grow the weeds that are undesirable.

Judging from the products many people are harvesting, their minds must resemble neglected victory gardens.

PMA Science of Success, Educational Edition. Napoleon Hill Foundation, 1961, p. 32.

Action Assignment #29

Accentuate the Positive — Eliminate the Negative!

This is a title of an old song with very valuable contemporary advice. Remove old recordings in your sub-conscious mind by erasing, scratching, blasting, evaporating, or de-materializing — whatever annihilation method works best - the old "program" that you no longer care to run.

Next, supplant with well-constructed new programs following the lesson given by Jack Boland in this week's ezine. Today, create ten positive affirmations that will replace those old, offensive recordings that keep you falling in life's potholes. Today, get unstuck and hitch your wagon to the start of the new and improved version of yourself that will endure for a lifetime. TRULY, be your very best always and in all ways beginning right now, today! No excuses! Only you can change you. Disengage your automatic pilot and take hands on control of your instrument panel. It is your course now. What direction will you take?

Chapter 30

Achieving goals can make you happy—very happy. But only if the goals are part of a larger purpose and if they are your own *goals.*
– Arnold Fox & Barry Fox

Most things that we need to be self-sufficient have a monetary price tag. Food, shelter, and clothing are requirements that we should provide for ourselves via work. The price of these basic needs vary in degree, but usually cost us something. Still, a good portion of these things remain unaffordable for many people of the earth. It is true. It costs to live on this planet and we must provide ourselves with the daily necessities of life through our earnings. This is a simple fact of life.

Conversely, some luxuries in life are priceless and not for sale for any amount. Let's list a few. Think about your allotted lifespan, the ancestors you inherited, your immediate family, the song of a robin, the scent of new mown grass, the loyalty of a pet, the sun, the moon, the stars, the air you breathe, the ground you walk on, the water you drink, the friendship of a loyal person, the taste of favorite foods, the scent of a lilac, the sight of a double rainbow, the sound of your child's voice, and the touch of a feather.

In an instant, anyone could lose the opportunity to experience these things through illness or death, but they are sensory jewels given to us by the Creator to allow us to experience joy without cost each day. Money and financial security are nice to have but without the equal distribution of the abstract goodness life has to offer anyone would be truly bankrupt. Little things do mean a lot. Consider whether or not you would want to live with all the wealth in the world, but not have access to the joys of living. I would think that you would not.

So, as we weigh the cost effectiveness of living, let's consider the beauty, wonder, and richness that life offers to each one of us daily. Instead of demanding more of ourselves as we work, why do we not demand more of ourselves as we live? Free time is necessary and renews our instincts to survive. Life without a positive attitude toward living is no life at all. We need balance and the wisdom to know when we have depleted the resources in our energy storehouse. Once renewed through downtime, vacation, recess, or play we can begin again to offer the world the richness of our talents and resources. If not renewed by taking time for ourselves we become resentful, embittered, shallow, and like a well that has run dry. Before this happens, make certain that you are balancing your life so that the joy of living shines through in your daily work. Balance in life is the key to long term positive results.

In speaking with James Oleson, the President of The Napoleon Hill Foundation, he states: "Sometimes you have to slow down and go fishing." Jim knows how to balance play with work!

Rhythms in Relaxation

by Napoleon Hill

Relaxation means the complete forgetting of the worries and problems of the day. Yet there is a constant stream of people who need to relax who in effect say, "Doctor, I cannot relax." Surprising as this seems, this is probably true, since relaxing is a negative quality.

Let me see if I can make this clear: the conscious mind is, among other things, a selecting mechanism. We select things we like to concentrate upon. The act of concentration implies exclusion of other thoughts. We cannot concentrate on flying kites, growing roses or any other hobby unless we are fascinated by the field. If we are, it occupies all our thoughts and feelings when we get on the subject. At that moment we have forgotten the worries and problems of the day; we are relaxing.

Haven't we all had the experience of meeting a depressed, worried individual and attempting to find his pet subject of conversation, whether it be baseball, badminton or business? When we strike his real interest, this depressed, morose face, full of worry and frustration, lights up, becomes animated, charming and interesting. His frown is shed like the cocoon of a butterfly. It is hard to believe this is the same person who was so dejected a moment before. His mind is no longer focused on his worries, but now on another real interest. *He has stopped worrying and begun to play.* He has also given his subconscious mind a chance to solve his problems, *while he was playing. This is truly relaxing.*

PMA Science of Success, Educational Edition. Napoleon Hill Foundation, 1961, pp. 439–440.

Action Assignment #30

Take time for fun. What activities do you take part in? Look at active activities, not passive ones. How you use your free time now will contribute to your problem solving ability, peace of mind, and longevity. Because relaxation refreshes the mind and body, a person cannot afford to not relax. Seek hobbies and interests that are diverse. Go where your imagination leads you. List seven things that you would enjoy doing if given the time. Entertainment does not count since it is mostly passive. List only those things that you possess a desire to know more about and to become actively involved in doing. For example, I am interested in learning more about papier-mâché, refurbishing old furniture, gardening, cooking, and cats. What are your inclinations? Begin to focus on one or more now and see where it leads.

Chapter 31

I'll never forget the thrill I got when I read a book filled with tremendous truths that were completely opposite to what I had believed.

– Charlie "Tremendous" Jones

Biographies are a good way to learn about a person's life and apply the teachings to our own situation. "Take the best and leave the rest" is good advice when reading for ideas and practices that one can immediately use today.

Biographies come in all shapes and sizes. Here are a few categories that may captivate your interest: Developing Leadership, Teaching and Sharing, Promoting Peace, Helping and Healing, Overcoming Obstacles, Finding Courage, and Providing Comfort and Solace to others. Just give any librarian one or more of these categories and you will be led to discover books whose stories may captivate you for years to come.

If you read from more than one category, it will expand your awareness about what life has to offer—social, emotional, physical, financial, mental, and spiritual are other ways of looking at the divergent paths taken by many who come before us and leave a lesson after they are gone. By reading a biography on St. Francis, Abraham Lincoln, Andrew Carnegie, Albert Einstein, Helen Keller, Clark Gable, Gandhi, Harriet Beecher Stowe and Richard Nixon we can expand not only our awareness of the world, but also entire areas of living that at first glance may not have appealed to us.

Do people really read biographies and use the guidance they bring in the printed word? Well, the ones I just mentioned above are biographies that W. Clement Stone read and kept in his personal library. He enjoyed the stories of people's lives because they gave him tips on how better to live his own. I imagine that he read the lives of those people he admired and learned a great deal in the process.

Another friend of Great Books was Charlie T. Jones. I have had the pleasure of hearing him speak several times, and I always laughed when he gave his favorite books a big kiss in front of the audience. He loved to read, and he read good books. Consider reading Charlie's *Life is Tremendous* for an optimistic look at life for today. You just may begin to kiss books too!

Also, you might also want to consider Don Green's book, *Everything I Know About Success I Learned from Napoleon Hill.* In his book, Don details events in his life that helped him aspire to achieve great things for both himself and others. Don enjoys sharing information in a story fashion and personally I enjoy hearing the tales about his growing up years in Wise. I can just imagine what his mother had to say when he came home not only with a monkey, but even a bear too! And a bear that liked Little Debbie Cakes to boot! But, there is a limit to everything, and I would have put my foot down when the snakes appeared. So, Don's saga is an interesting one! Read the book and you will be entertained and perhaps inspired to write down your life's history as well.

Why not explore a life well lived today? Go back in time—a year, a decade, a century, or more, and learn from a person you have always admired but may need to know more about. Become an expert on the life of someone who can reach across the pages of a book and still touch you in your life today. Their legacy exists to be shared with you right now—when you open the book. So open that book or load that e-book and begin to be enlightened, inspired, and invigorated by a person who selflessly shares their lesson in living through their life stories.

Educational Activity

by Napoleon Hill

No man is ever through learning. If your major purpose in life is aimed above the average, you must continue to learn from every possible source, and especially when you can acquire knowledge particularly related to your purpose. Books in the public library make available to you the entire accumulated experience of mankind all highly organized and presented to you in concise forms. All they require of you in return is your effort in reading and studying them. Another source of knowledge and information too often overlooked is found in your daily life. By carefully choosing your friends and associates you can acquire a liberal education in a variety of subjects by the very enjoyable medium of conversation. This is a rich source of help, and one that you can tap by carefully selecting a social master mind group who will find the exchange mutually beneficial.

PMA Science of Success, Educational Edition. Napoleon Hill Foundation, 1961, pp. 71–72.

Action Assignment #31

Go online, to the library, or to your personal collection of books.

Locate, list, and read one book in each of the sections that I mentioned above. You should have a list of 7 or more when you finish. Make these selected persons your imaginary counselors, as Dr. Hill calls them, for now. As you read, list characteristics that you would like to emulate in your life. You do not have to read them all at once, nor would I suggest that you do that. But, begin with one, read through it, and become familiar with the person who you are reading about. Next, list the positive attributes that you want to acquire that this person possesses. Then, go to the next book and do the same. Look at this as your summer reading list. When you finish all seven or more, you will definitely be an improved version of yourself! And, you may even want to thank the other person you read about, mentally or otherwise.

Enjoy the books!

CHAPTER 32

Some souls there are that needs must taste
of wrong, ere choosing right;
we should not call those years a waste
which led us to the light.

– *Ella Wheeler Wilcox*

The story about the humane capture of monkeys in Africa is a favorite of mine because it holds a valuable lesson for each of us regarding possessions. The story goes that some food is placed in a container that has an opening big enough for the monkey's paw. When the monkey reaches in and grabs the nuts, banana, or special treat it makes a fist as it grasps the food. Reluctant to release the treat, it is captured because it won't loosen its grip. The "trap" is too heavy to carry around thereby the monkey is caught. If the monkey would just open its paw it would be free to go.

The relevance of this story to our lives is too important to pass up. We can carry around our problems figuratively and stubbornly refuse to give them up. When help is offered, we tighten our grip and hold on tightly afraid of what might happen if we release our concerns. This action alone prevents many people from becoming who they might have been. Arrogantly knowing what is best stops people from ever acquiring anything better.

Physically, the monkey's paw can represent our possessions too. Afraid to release what we have to those who could put it to a better use we hang on tenaciously until our possessions control us and not vice versa. Once we realize that, like the monkey, we have to release the hold we have on things before the Universe can bring freedom into our lives. It is a difficult lesson to learn, but one that can open up opportunities for us in the future. If we remain caught then we never advance to the new life that could be waiting for us.

So as we reflect on the monkey story, think about anything in your life that inhibits your growth or freedom. As with the monkey, it occurs because you allow it to occur. By acknowledging our greed, arrogance, or hunger, we can begin to realize that if we let go and perhaps delay our gratification for a time there might be two bananas instead of one waiting for us a la carte. Seriously, when we lessen our stronghold on life it often surprises us by bringing to the banquet table all the good life has to offer.

Advantages of Defeat

by Napoleon Hill

Defeat may have the effect of supplanting vanity and arrogance with humility of heart, thus paving the way for the formation of more harmonious human relationships. It may cause you to take self-inventory and to uncover the weakness which brought about your defeat.

Defeat may lead to the development of a stronger willpower, provided you accept it as a challenge to greater effort and not as a signal to stop trying. This is perhaps the greatest potential benefit to be found in defeat, because the seed of equivalent benefit which exists in the circumstances of all defeat abides entirely in your own mental attitude. It is therefore, under your control.

You may not always control the outward effects of defeat, if it involves the loss of material things or damages other people, but you can control your own reaction to the experience and profit by it.

PMA Science of Success, Educational Edition. Napoleon Hill Foundation, 1961, pp. 391–392.

Action Assignment #32

Reflect for a few minutes on how you may be contributing to an impasse or two in your life.

Although it is hard to admit that we could be part of the problem, when we admit our compliance we advance forward to new horizons. When we clench our hand into a fist, we remain deadlocked right where we are. Today, when a problem faces you, consider how you might be a co-conspirator in prolonging or maintaining the problem. Assess the six areas of your life where this can occur—mental, spiritual, social, emotional, physical, and financial. These few moments of looking within could and very often do help you address the problem head-on and then work towards its dissolution.

Chapter 33

Unless you figure out which fears are plaguing you and come up with a workable plan to conquer and control them once and for all, they will always lurk close by, ready to inject themselves into your everyday life.

– T. W. Walker

Offer it up! Walk a mile in someone else's moccasins. Be truthful. Be patient. Think of others first. Be a giver, not a taker. And on and on....

All these pieces of advice, and other good ones not listed above, tell us in a commanding manner to practice the Golden Rule. Giving begets giving, and selfishness creates a bottleneck in the process. It all comes down to whether we think of ourselves first or someone else. This is not intended to mean that we become a patsy or a victim of the will of others, but that we truly see a need and work to fill it with no thought of recompense. Hard to do, but being of service to others is the only way to get the gold stars in Heaven's grade book. The difficult part—the discernment—is how much to do for someone else before you are being taken advantage of and serving as a slave and not as a benefactor. Many people will let you offer the gift that keeps on giving—yourself—and they are very happy to be the recipient of your generosity. You will have to decide when this is happening and if you are being used or useful. Only you can make this judgment.

Charity begins at home. This saying may well be the other side of the coin to consider when giving because we can just as easily be the recipient of our own largess. Nothing is more important than this day. Have you slowed down enough to enjoy it? Have you opened your eyes to the moment and thanked the Universe for giving you the opportunity to experience the green grass, the beautiful hummingbird, the monarch butterfly, the flower scented breeze, the porch swing, and more? Well, you should because these are all priceless gifts from above that each of us can afford but seldom find time to enjoy.

Now is the time to slow down to the speed of summer and rest in the earth's loveliness. Who is counting, but how many summers do you think you have left? Could be your last chance to give yourself this very special gift. As W. Clement Stone states, "Do it now!" You, and others, will be the better for it. Proper rest insures greater productivity. Give yourself permission to take a break. Afterwards, assess your productivity. Greater, right? Because you decided to be of service to yourself first and then offer your service to others. You can't fill a jug from an empty well. Replenish yourself by giving to yourself first when you feel that you may be running dry.

What is the Golden Rule—Really?

by Napoleon Hill

We should not content ourselves with the merest crumbs from life's table, and we should not attempt to grab too much. The Golden Rule often seems to act as a great leveler in assuring that this shall be so. It creates an ever-present spirit of kindly consideration for the needs and rights of others, so that without thought of gain (which so often is twisted by small minds into grabbing) the mind infused with the Golden Rule acquires a sense of what constitutes its own true ability to give. Giving begets receiving: there is a to-and-fro passage of wealth which may not reflect itself in a swollen bank account, but does reflect itself in a mind which has known such wealth. In this lies happiness, peace and health which a man merely rich in money may never know.

Grow Rich With Peace of Mind. Ballantine Books, 1996, pp. 185–186.

Action Assignment #33

This week's assignment comes to you from the desk of Napoleon Hill. It is a great fit with the readings for this week, and good philosophical food for thought. Read on and then journal your responses, ideas, thoughts as you consider what Dr. Hill has to say to each of us below.

A suggestion: Look around in your community and find some man who you know lives for the purpose of accumulating money. Find some man—and alas, you can find such men—for whom any amount of money is too little and no amount is too much. He will almost certainly be a man who has little conscience about how he acquires his money, for conscience can be a hindrance when your horizon is nothing but a line of empty money bags to be filled.

Observe this man. Look for warmth in his soul; you will not find it, unless the subject of discussion is money. Watch for a warm, human welcome in his smile; you will not see it—he smiles like a shark. Notice how little he displays an enjoyment of life. Oh, he may go through various expensive motions of enjoyment, but that is something else again. In the humane sense of the word, such a man is not really human. He is an automaton—a money-making machine. Yet many will envy that mechanical man. They will point to what they call his success.

Can there be success without happiness? Any really human person knows the two must go together as partners in a worthwhile life. No man who thinks that happiness lies in having too much ever will be happy. No man can be truly happy until he translates the words of the Golden Rule into deeds, and shares happiness with others. Moreover, the Golden Rule was not meant to be enforced like taxes. The sharing of happiness brings happiness when the sharing is voluntary, with no other object than to give.

Grow Rich With Peace of Mind. Ballantine Books, 1996, p. 186.

CHAPTER 34

I believe many things in my life were achieved through a combination of success principles used with enthusiasm. Just like it takes more than one ingredient for a recipe to be tasty, success takes more than one principle of success, stirred vigorously with enthusiasm.

– Gayle Washausen

Life is precious. We often overlook this reality in the daily duties and commitments of living. People we love and care for are placed in the "always have been and always will be" status in our minds, and we overlook the timelines that we are forced to confront when someone dies. Afterwards we may feel guilt and remorse because we lost contact or did not maintain contact as we now wish we had. Some family members stay close and others become distant. Friends too shift in the same manner. Life exists in a state of constant renewal and no matter how we would like to keep things the same, everything changes but the memories do linger.

Memories are a blessing and they can be recalled and created as well. One of my favorite Biblical verses is "Behold, I make all things new." Living in the past prevents us from expanding to our future. Our lifespan and purpose may synchronize with another's for a period of time, and then it may diverge. This is not to say that we were on the wrong path or distanced ourselves from friends and family, but rather to acknowledge the fluid nature of living. Our life goes on, even when it stops for others.

While visiting my sister in Florida, I had the opportunity to walk a small labyrinth one morning. As the paths turned, large rocks with messages were placed at several points for reflection. The following were the messages: *Your life is a journey, not a destination.... Reconnect with your mind.... Listen for guidance.... Deepen your compassion.... Increase your patience.... Set an intention.... Ask a question.... Reflect on a dream..... Remember a friend.... Come to terms.*

Living allows us to remember where we have been and then to progress to where we are going. Napoleon Hill reminds us that nature abhors a vacuum and soon will fill it. And, he also tells us that all energy exists now—it is neither created nor destroyed but continually changes from one from to another. As changes in our lives occur, it is essential to remember to acknowledge the past for the gifts given to us and to journey toward the future since we are here to aspire to whatever possibilities are waiting for us.

A Letter Can Change a Life for the Better

by W. Clement Stone & Napoleon Hill

Now faith can be expressed in a letter. In fact, a letter is an excellent tool for expressing one's thoughts and motivating another person.

A letter can change a life for the better. Anyone who writes a letter affects the subconscious mind of the receiver through suggestion. And the power of this suggestion is, of course, dependent upon several factors.

If you are a parent, for example, and your son or daughter is away at school, you can accomplish that which you might not otherwise achieve. You can grasp the opportunity: (a) to mold the character of your child; (b) to discuss matters that you might hesitate or never take the time to discuss in conversation; and (c) to express your inner thoughts.

Now a boy or girl may not readily accept advice when it is given verbally. For environment and emotions involved at the time of the conversation might prevent this. And yet the same boy or girl would treasure the same advice received in a carefully written, sincere letter.

To a son or daughter away from home a letter with all of its content, including advice, is most welcome. And if it is properly written, it may be read frequently, studied, and digested.

Success Through a Positive Mental Attitude. Napoleon Hill & W. Clement Stone, Prentice-Hall, 1960, pp. 113–114.

Action Assignment #34

Reflect on the messages carved in stone as you walk a labyrinth or take a simple circular nature walk.

The messages are:

1. Your life is a journey, not a destination.
2. Reconnect with your mind.
3. Listen for guidance.
4. Deepen your compassion.
5. Increase your patience.
6. Set an intention.
7. Ask a question.
8. Reflect on a dream.
9. Remember a friend.
10. Come to terms.

As you spend time in reflection, consider the thoughts that come to mind and expand on the two most significant ideas for you today and discuss your feelings with another, journal your responses, or simply thank the Universe for making you aware of these messages carved in stone. This is a form of meditation and it will give you an opportunity to quiet your monkey mind and consider what really matters.

Chapter 35

You can change from negative to positive thinking and enjoy all the blessings that follow such a change. This is possible no matter how long and how completely you have been a negative-thinking person.

– Norman Vincent Peale

Having little quotations at the ready for difficult situations provides us with a mental antidote for any negativity that may appear in life. If memorized, these autosuggestions are employed to ease our mind and calm our emotions when we encounter life's ups and downs. Dr. Hill's work is full of many sayings that offer support when a person needs a boost in their positive mental attitude. It is good to commit those sayings of our own choosing to memory since they will then remind us of the direction we have set as our course in life. Also, by selecting ones that appeal to us, we are more likely to use them for a positive end result.

In *Success Through a Positive Mental Attitude,* by Hill and W. Clement Stone, Biblical quotes recommended by Dr. Peale are quoted. They are:

- As he thinketh in his heart, so is he.
- If thou canst believe, all things are possible to him that believeth.
- Lord, I believe; help Thou mine unbelief!
- According to your faith be it unto you.
- Faith without works is dead.
- What things soever ye desire, when ye pray, believe that ye receive them, and ye shall have them.
- If God be for us, who can be against us?
- Ask and it shall be given you; seek and ye shall find; knock, and it shall be opened unto you.

I admit that I use thought conditioners like these almost daily for a variety of things. If I am stressed, tired, unable to sleep, stymied, impatient, angry, hateful, belligerent, uneasy, fretful, confused, or just looking for direction I allow some of my favorite sayings to come to mind. Somehow these quotations can soothe like a caress when life becomes difficult.

Driving to work I see a billboard that gives me pause. It asks: "What's the difference between an abusive parent and one who isn't? About 7–10 seconds." The difference in reality is the matter of seconds that it takes to reflect on an action that can or cannot be taken. Parents who reflect on what they may or may not do to a child in anger think the better of it when they pause to consider what they are about to do. Thinking through situations often allows a person to cool down and respond with a higher degree of control. Thinking puts us back in control of our emotions, and thought conditioners help us to pause, regain control, and then act instead of react. My advice to you is to take the best and leave the rest. If it works for you, use it!

Mental Cobwebs

by Napoleon Hill

1. Negative: (a) feelings, (b) emotions, and (c) passions; (d) habits, (e) beliefs, and (f) prejudices.
2. Seeing only the mote in the other fellow's eye.
3. Arguments and misunderstandings due to semantic difficulties.
4. False conclusions resulting from false premises.
5. All-inclusive, restrictive words or expressions as basic or minor premises.
6. The idea that necessity forces dishonesty.
7. Unclean thoughts and habits.
8. Fear that it is sacrilegious to use the powers of your mind.

And so you see there are many varieties of cobwebs—some small, some large, some weak, some strong. Yet if you make an additional listing of your own, and then examine the strands of each cobweb closely, you will find that they are all spun by NMA [negative mental attitude].

And when you think about it for a while, you will see that the strongest cobweb spun by NMA is the cobweb of inertia. Inertia causes you to do nothing; or, if you are moving in the wrong direction, keeps you from resisting or stopping.

Success Through a Positive Mental Attitude. Napoleon Hill & W. Clement Stone, Prentice-Hall, 1960, pp. 40–41.

Action Assignment #35

Clean out your mental cobwebs. Analyze your thought starters and thought conditioners. Determine what contributes to making your attitude negative or positive.

Take a close, personal, sincere look at yourself and at your thoughts that have made you who you are today. Do you like what you see? That's good if the answer is yes, and that's good if the answer is no, because *you* have the capacity to make or remake yourself to your personal satisfaction. This week, do some soul searching in order to determine what qualities you possess.

Next, begin to work on those qualities that you want to change by locating positive quotations that support your goal. Select ten powerful ones and memorize them. When you arrive at a crossroads and you begin to repeat behaviors you no longer desire, remake your action by mentally reciting the quotation that best fits the situation. The recitation should be by rote, and repeated, and repeated, and repeated.

Very soon you will notice a change for the better in your behavior. When you notice this you will have successfully begun to create a new pattern and erase the old one.

Chapter 36

No one among us stands alone. The success you enjoy today and the vision that you have for tomorrow only exists because you have been privileged to stand on the shoulders of giants.

– Jim Stovall

The weather seems to be turning quickly to fall here in Northwest Indiana, U.S.A., and the season of harvest is upon us. I am always amazed at the enormous quantity of apples, grapes, tomatoes, and pears that my small fruit trees and home garden produces this time of year. Just seeing the apple tree bending beneath the weight of the apples reminds me of the abundance that is promised to those who plant good seeds! Nature always goes beyond our expectations in delivering results!

Dr. Hill states: "You will find that nature goes the extra mile in everything she does. She does not create just enough of each genus or specie to get by, but rather produces an overabundance to take care of all emergencies which may arise and still guarantee the perpetuation of each form of life."

When we place our trust and confidence in Nature, we are borrowing good will. Businesses can do the same to prosper. When a business establishes satisfactory dealings with others over time confidence is created in their product. By practicing sound business techniques that include honest and trustworthy relationships, good will flourishes. Just as with Nature, an overabundance ensues and the business expands.

Life delivers good things to those who work toward the good. An ingredient that encourages this abundance and functions much like a fertilizer does for plants is gratitude. Expressing our heartfelt gratitude for what we already have predisposes us to receive more. When our attention is placed upon what is good, our inner space expands and room for more is created.

This season, look around you and see the beauty and expansiveness of Nature in all its glory. You too are a product of this Universe, and not only can you appreciate the glory around you but you can call it forward in your own life through acknowledging the gifts that you have been given. Gratitude grows when you fertilize it. You fertilize it by accepting the gifts that you have been given, and passing them on to others. Use your ability to make life better for someone else, and your life will blossom as a result.

Active Faith

by Napoleon Hill

Before the state of mind known as faith will produce practical results, it must be expressed in some form of action.

> Faith without works is dead.
>
> *–James 2:20*

Have you ever kept a little garden spot of your own and had the experience of raising things? Anyone who has kept a garden knows that keeping out the weeds is a continual job. Somehow the weeds seem to grow a little faster than the vegetables or flowers. You have to adopt whatever measures you find effective to fight those weeds, while at the same time watering, fertilizing and cultivating the vegetables and flowers. The same thing goes on in your mind. It will grow you a rich crop, but you have to keep the soil planted with seeds of thought concerning those things you desire, and make certain that they get plenty of the sunshine of your faith to bring them to fruition. At the same time you must be diligent in the elimination of the weeds of fear, doubt, discouragement and thoughts of self-limitation.

Here is a poem which expresses these ideas most beautifully:

Our prayers are answered; each unspoken thought
And each desire implanted in the mind
Bears its own harvest, after its own kind;
Who dreams of beauty has already caught
The flash of angel wings. Who seeks to find
True wisdom shall assuredly be taught.
But thorns of fate have thorny thoughts behind;
For out of our own hearts our lives are wrought.
Be on thy guard, my soul, lest wind-blown seed
Into the fertile soil of thought should fall
And lodging place within the garden wall
Be given to bitter rue or noxious weed.
Unspoken prayers bear fruitage. Love thoughts call
Forth into being every loving deed.
Idle or earnest, still our prayers are all
Answered according to our inward creed.

–*Bonnie Day*

PMA Science of Success, Educational Edition. Napoleon Hill Foundation, 1961, pp. 105–106.

Action Assignment #36

Recite Napoleon Hill's Prayer of Gratitude three times daily, morning, noon, and night, and notice your results. Focus on what you are grateful for in your life, and be aware of how your gratitude affects your awareness.

> I give thanks daily, not for mere riches, but for wisdom with which to recognize, embrace, and properly use the great abundance of riches I now have at my command. I have no enemies because I injure no man for any cause, but I try to benefit all with whom I come in contact, by teaching them the way to enduring riches. I have more material wealth than I need because I am free from greed and covet only the material things I can use while I live.
>
> – Napoleon Hill

Chapter 37

Security in a relationship lies neither in looking back to what it was in nostalgia, nor forward to what it might be in dread or anticipation, but living in the present relationship and accepting it as it is now.

– Anne Morrow Lindbergh

Life is impermanent on this plane of existence. We need to make the best of it while we have it. To me it seems that our incarnation in this world is much like that of a caterpillar inching toward its final imprisonment in its lonely cocoon. However, what initially may appear like death shortly results in a magnificent rebirth as a glorious, winged butterfly. Who is to say that our life after life won't be the same wonderful miracle of transformation? We will just have to wait and see. Let's anticipate it as we do our early birthdays, not dread it as some ominous departure date that will gobble us up! The choice of attitude is ours alone.

Napoleon Hill has taught us in his works to witness the laws of Cosmic Habitforce in their constancy. If we do this, we can see time after time the replication of life in all things. Old ways die and new ones are born, yet everything remains the same. Why wouldn't Nature treat us the same? It only makes logical sense that this process will occur for us too.

In the meantime, the NOW of our existence, let's celebrate the beauty of life and live in the current moment. It takes an attitude adjustment to do this continually, but we have been given that gift of choice as our divine inheritance. We can choose life each moment, and not whittle our time away in nostalgia, mourning, or regret. As humans, we grow through education, and endure because as our level of consciousness is raised through personal reflection and spiritual growth, so too is our quality of life.

Live each day you have been given to enjoy, and make peace with what is to come because we do not control our coming in or our going out. But, we do control all the moments in between. Make the most of the journey. One of my favorite quotations is by Goethe. He states, "Whatever you can do, or dream you can, begin it. Boldness has genius, power, and magic in it." Dream it and make all your sweet dreams come true.

Your Source of Power

by Napoleon Hill

Before the state of mind known as faith will produce practical results, it must be expressed in some form of action. I wonder how many people know the number of failures the average man can survive without quitting and giving up the ghost in despair. To satisfy my curiosity on this subject I once made a survey through which I examined men and women to ascertain their staying qualities in the face of failure or defeat.

The majority of them quit trying when overtaken one time by defeat. A very small percentage of them kept on trying a second time. But by far the greater number quit even before meeting with defeat because they expected it and quit before they really started.

Needless to suggest, there were no Edisons and no Fords in this group.

They were the average run-of-the-mill of humanity who somehow never got around to recognizing the master key to riches with which they were endowed at birth: a master key consisting of their ability to tune in and appropriate the power of Infinite Intelligence by the simple process of conditioning their minds to receive and use this great universal power.

A Treasury of Success Unlimited. The Napoleon Hill Foundation, 2008, p. 88.

Action Assignment #37

Do something special for someone else.

Look through a box of old photos, or even an old cd of photos, and find one of someone who needs a pick-me-up. Select the "moment in time photo," have it copied and enlarged, and put it in a special frame. You can even create the frame yourself to match the scene in the picture. If it includes a seaside, add shells and sand. If it depicts a fall scene, add leaves and acorns. You get the idea. It does not have to include you—just the person you are remembering.

Next, write a brief note indicating what the photo means to you and why you are happy to share it with the person in the photo. This gift of giving a happy memory just might recondition an old relationship and make someone happier as well. Notice where and how the person displays your creation from the heart next time you visit them too!

Chapter 38

There is a pattern of perfection at the center of your being which has never been touched by disease or misfortune. Your intellect senses this through intuition, your imagination feels it by divine right, your inward consciousness knows it through faith.

– Ernest Holmes

What is it that each of us can do to stop the violence in today's world? Is this an unanswerable question, or is there a solution? Daily, innocent lives are impacted by another's negative tendencies, and we are all left to wonder what can be done. Surely, the cause has to be the negative emotions run amok that Napoleon Hill discusses in his teachings. They are: Fear, Hatred, Anger, Envy, Greed, Jealousy, Revenge, Irritability, and Superstition. These negative emotions are capable of being brought under control through the exercise of reason and self-discipline. If not, they can escalate into dangerous and destructive actions. First, however, people must be educated in order to do this. It is not an inherited response, but rather an acquired, learned one.

Emotions need to be harnessed and channeled into a constructive force that aids in the attainment of a definite major purpose. Too often it seems that emotions are not channeled or regulated, and chaos results. It seems that when individuals have nothing constructive to focus on in their lives, some turn to counterproductive measures as we have recently seen in the news.

The seed of negativity becomes full blown when life's mission is skewed. Having no purpose and no plan results in lives of not-so-quiet desperation—and this negativity impacts us all. By embracing the dark side of life, drifters assume they will gain the recognition that they are unable to achieve by other means. Going back to the source or seedling of the problem challenges all of us to help others identify their lifelong purpose.

As fellow travelers on this journey, we are obliged to assist others that need support. Instead of ignoring the wanderer, offer assistance by listening and then guidance. Perhaps by being a mentor rather than a bystander, some of the violence can be reduced. As the saying goes, if we light just one small candle we can begin to eradicate the darkness. If we listen more than we talk, discuss more than we condemn, and seek avenues for inclusion rather than exclusion, steps to solving the problem can be undertaken together. In order to make the world a better place in which to live, each person has to begin within themselves. Otherwise, the violence will continue and it will become a common occurrence that we will have to endure more often than not.

My Day's Work Is Over

by Napoleon Hill

My Day's work is over and I am ready to relax my body in sleep. I have summoned my Cabinet of imaginary Counselors around me that I may consult their master minds in planning for the morrow.

I can all but hear the immortal Shakespeare who sits at my right, as he says: "To thine own self be true and it must follow as the night the day, thou canst not then be false to any man."

And, I can all but hear Lincoln, who sits at my left, as he says: "With charity for all and malice toward none."

And, I can all but hear proud old Socrates as he says: "And you, too, judges, must face death with a good courage, and believe this as a truth, that no evil can happen to a good man, either in life or after death."

And, I can all but hear that master philosopher, Emerson, as he says: "Nothing can bring you peace but yourself. Nothing can bring you peace but the triumph of principles."

And, I can all but hear the Man of Galilee as he says: "Therefore all things whatsoever ye would that men should do to you, do ye even so to them."

The Counsel Table around which I gather, with these great men of the past each night, is an imaginary one, but the messages which they left behind them are real, and I am using this method of burning them deeply into my consciousness, that their influence may find its way into the pattern after which my character is being built.

Napoleon Hill's Magazine. Vol. I, No. 5 (September, 1921), Back Cover.

Action Assignment #38

The idea of a "message in a bottle" is intriguing and speaks to many of us about something reaching us from outside of our comfort zone.

When a bottle washes ashore, the finder eagerly uncorks it to reveal something inside that may harbor a specific message intended for the recipient. Written messages are real and can be found in many places such as books, on monuments, in letters, and anywhere else the written word is preserved. Just as Napoleon Hill was inspired by thoughts written down and preserved, you too can recall and capture famous thoughts that help you build the character you desire. These quotations are not simply platitudes if they speak to you. Rather, they are like mental vitamins that will strengthen your character, improve your mental physique, and support your spiritual strength as you reflect on how these ideas contribute to your well-being.

Today, gather your favorite ten written messages that you will recite daily to improve your life. Look for new thoughts to inspire you, and when found, copy down the saying. Next, give it renewed life. Recite it in your own voice, and thereby internalize it as you would nourishing food. Thoughts sustain too—they sustain our character and mold who we are becoming. Think good thoughts. Just like an apple a day, they keep our mental system tuned up!

Chapter 39

The Golden Rule: Treat others the way you *want to be treated and help others the way* you *would want someone to help you. We can do better and we must do better, and you can make a difference by being proactive and prevention-focused.*

– Rick Shaw

Rather than notice the flaws in others, why not notice the beauty? People tend to nitpick at what is wrong instead of appreciate what is right. Consider that in handcrafting their beautiful quilts, the Amish intentionally create a flaw in the piece to indicate that the only perfect thing in the universe is the Creator. In weaving, the Navajo do something similar. They leave an opening in the blanket or piece to allow Spirit to flow through. Each community of believers intends to give credit to the Force that is behind Creation by acknowledging that our individual work exists because we have been given the opportunity to create ourselves from a greater Source.

In discussing Creative Imagination, Dr. Hill advocates keeping our eyes open and drawing from our own external experiences and then capitalizing upon these experiences as we allow them to linger in both our waking and sleeping worlds. From these ingredients we can then gift back to the Universe our personalized creation that is uniquely ours.

The poet Robert Browning wrote:

O would some power the gift to give us
to see ourselves as others see us.

I agree with Browning in asking for the grace to see ourselves as we are seen by others. Also, it would be good to anticipate that others can see us for who we truly are by the gifts we create and share with the world. This loop can help each of us create our own original masterpiece by drawing from the external world and then giving back to it from our innate talents.

Why not begin with exploring imagination as Dr. Hill explains it? He states: "Creative vision has its base in the spirit of the universe which expresses itself through the brain of man." As we envision ourselves as a container for spirit that seeks expression through each of us, the divine light shines forth via our talents!

What is it you desire to create or manifest in your life? Is it good? If so, let your little light shine and illuminate the world by giving the gift of yourself to others.

Edison, the Electric Light Bulb, and Synthetic Imagination

by Napoleon Hill

Nature yields her most profound secrets to the man who is determined to uncover them.

When Edison thought of the charcoal principle, his imagination immediately associated it with the other half of his idea—the heating of wire with electrical energy—and he recognized that the heat of the wire could be controlled by placing the wire inside a vacuum where the amount of oxygen reaching the heat could be controlled.

He placed the wire inside a bottle, pumped out most of the air, turned on the electric power, and the first practical incandescent electric lamp was born. The crude model burned for eight and a half hours. From that beginning came the modern electric light bulb. It was the beginning for the great age of electricity which was destined to change the habits of mankind throughout the world, because it laid the foundation for every electrical device used today, including modern radio and television tubes.

Mr. Edison carried on his experiments without financial support from others. He applied the principle of going the extra mile every step of the way, because he labored without immediate pay. He also worked with definiteness of purpose and was inspired by applied faith to carry on through a period of failures that would have turned back most men.

PMA Science of Success, Educational Edition. Napoleon Hill Foundation, 1961, p. 403.

Action Assignment #39

Ask someone to collect 20 to 25 ordinary small objects for you and place these everyday objects in a bag or box. Give yourself an hour to spread out the objects on a table before you.

Looking at each, consider their current use and then select two or three items from the group and consider how a combination of these items can be arranged so as to create a new item with a new use. Example would be the Eskimo Pie that Dr. Hill refers to — simply vanilla ice cream dipped in chocolate. Be silly or serious. You decide. I often marvel at the sticky note or Velcro products. Both were created from the inventors' imagination. Velcro evolved from observing Nature and sticky notes were a product that supposedly did not work. These two products are now used weekly if not daily by consumers. I would be willing to wager that you have both within your reach. I have the sticky notes on my desk and Velcro on the straps of my shoes. Can you find yours?

Chapter 40

We're all on a train going home. We're all born, and we're all going to die. Knowing when we die remains a mystery. But if, by chance, we did know the day we'd die, would it make a difference? Would we live life any differently?

– Julie Dankovich

Autumn is a time for slowing down and assessing what we have accomplished to date. Reviewing books we have read this year, movies we have watched, courses we have participated in, and goals we have met, are all points of reflection that help us gauge our progress by our own standards. The yardstick we use to measure is of our own creation, and the items we measure are ones we choose, but I often wonder if we should kick up our standards a notch or two?

The idea of moving beyond our comfort zone is a good one because that is where we can expand our horizons. If we always read the same genre of book, view the same type of movie, study the same materials, and stick to the same map sooner or later we will find that we are fully entrenched in a ditch we have dug by our choices. Although for some this does not seem a "bad" thing, over time our choices become enduring habits that lead us down a path that determines our destiny. Instead of repeating what we know, why not take a detour and experience a new way of doing something even though it may be uncomfortable and not the norm for us?

Instead of reading the latest and greatest fiction novel, why not ask someone you admire what book they can recommend as a good choice to read? Instead of seeing the type of movie that you prefer, why not see something educational that entertains as well as enlightens? Instead of frequenting the same restaurants, why not try a local eatery that focuses on ethnic food that you have not tried before? The choices for expansion are endless and they are as close by as a search on the internet. You do not have to do something unique daily, but once a week would give you 52 new experiences yearly and surely some would be "keepers" that you would continue to use.

Life is about living to the fullest, not becoming stuck in a rut. If happiness and enthusiasm are distant reminders of things you once did and enjoyed then it is time to rethink what you are doing. The past only has a stronghold on you if you permit it. As we mature and view the lifestyle we have created, it is only ourselves that hold us back from expanding and enhancing that lifestyle. Worry, fear, trepidation, and disenchantment with life are always lurking in the shadows and will overtake us if we allow it.

Likewise, happiness, goodness, and the riches of life are there too beckoning us to move forward. The choice and direction are ours. I hope that you choose life, now, in the moment, and live it to the fullest potential that is your birthright.

Close the Door on Your Past and Keep It Closed

by Napoleon Hill

I have heard it said that you never really get over the death of a loved one. This is so in the sense that every circumstance of your life, every joy and every sorrow, has an effect in shaping you into what you are. But you have great control over the way it shapes you—never forget that!

I am not one of those who believe in doing away with the natural emotion of sorrow when death occurs. Tears and sorrow are provided by nature as a safety valve for the overflowing emotions. Yet most people wait too long to close the door on mourning; or they never close it. We say: "There is no use in worrying over something you can't control." Yet we worry over death for unconscionable periods of time, knowing all the while we cannot control it.

The physical body comes from the air and the soil and goes back to the sources from which it came. Perhaps the mental and spiritual portions and some mysterious essence of life also go back to sources we can sense but cannot discover. So be it! Carry along with you not the pain you knew when a loved one died, but rather the positive and sustaining memories. As life is a natural process, so death is also.

Grow Rich With Peace of Mind. Ballantine, 1996, pp. 29–30.

Action Assignment #40

Put pen to paper and recall a life changing incident that offered you greater insight, passion, and upward expansion in your life. Your "essay" or recollection should be at least several pages.

As you delve into your remembrance, make certain that you capture the essence of the experience and why it has such significant meaning for you. Perhaps, you could pretend that you are seeing a counselor, minister, therapist, or good friend and you are relating this life changing experience to them one on one. Tell your story in detail, and leave nothing unsaid. This is therapeutic in more than one way. You are writing down a memory for posterity—if only for your eyes—and by sharing the event you are positioning it in time and now ready to more graciously beyond it. Grace has the capacity to move us beyond a point in time when otherwise we may become stuck. If the incident that you are writing about now is one that you frequently return to in your thoughts and dreams, it may just be the right moment to ground it and then bless it for the experience that it was, and move on. This story can either be shared or for your eyes only. The process of writing down a memory is the activity here. Sharing is optional and not required.

Chapter 41

If you know exactly what matters most to you, and what you really want to achieve not just in that moment, but in your life, it's easy to know whether a given thought is worth putting your time and energy into.

– Vic Conant

Have you ever been a victim of "stinkin' thinkin'?" This can happen when you allow uncontrolled enthusiasm to overrule accurate thinking. When you permit yourself to be persuaded that something is both factual and important without doing your own due diligence (aka *homework*) you are placing yourself in a precarious position. This can lead to harmful consequences if you allow yourself to be led blindly. Unguided, you just might plunge over the edge.

I personally know people who ask for advice and then do not accept it. What they really want is corroborating advice, advice that agrees with their own opinion. At times others may feel that they are receiving advice that is tainted with a person's own agenda, and that certainly can be true. However, it is easy to discern by determining if the person you are questioning has a vested, personal interest in what they are telling you or trying to sell you. If they do, then you need to find a trusted friend or associate who is outside their inner circle, and ask them the same question.

Sooner or later our belief in Santa Claus, the Easter Bunny, and the Tooth Fairy all come to a bittersweet end as we learn we have been hoodwinked into believing in a manufactured mythology. By staying little, we stay naïve. Many times substantiated facts are not pleasant but they provide a means by which we can evaluate our course of action. This new and improved course of action ultimately leads to our own destiny.

Mature adults are able to discern the accuracy of factual information. Dr. Hill provides us with the best tools for doing this repeatedly. By first taking action and researching the accuracy of what we are being told, next surveying trusted friends and associates for their views, and finally evaluating the total data for ourselves we are doing what works! It may be a slow process, but the end result is worth the effort. I would rather know the truth in the beginning than at the end after I have invested my time, resources and talent.

Young or old, the saying "there is no fool like an old fool" can apply to each and every one of us if we do not use the greatest gift the Creator has given to us, the power of thought. Through the accurate, organized use of this single gift we can shape and control our own lives.

Accurate Thinking

by Napoleon Hill

Everyone except the accurate thinker has an overabundance of opinions, and usually these are without great value. Many of them can also be dangerous and destructive when used in conjunction with personal initiative because if they are based upon bias, prejudice, intolerance, ignorance, guesswork or hearsay evidence, they may do a great deal of harm.

No opinion can be considered safe unless it is based upon known facts, and no one should express an opinion on any subject without assurance that it is founded on facts, or sound hypotheses of facts. Free advice volunteered by friends and acquaintances usually is not worthy of consideration. The accurate thinker, therefore, never acts upon such advice without giving it the closest scrutiny. Accurate thinkers permit no one to do their thinking for them. They obtain facts, information and counsel from others, but they retain the privilege of accepting or rejecting such advice in whole, or in part.

PMA Science of Success, Educational Edition. Napoleon Hill Foundation, 1961, pp. 299–300.

Action Assignment #41

Life can be full of past mistakes and regrets. These items can become excess emotional baggage that wear us down. By taking inventory of what works and what doesn't work in our lives, an improved pattern begins to develop that we can notice and cultivate.

For this week's activity follow in Dr. Hill's footsteps and become a reporter. Interview 10 people on the street or wherever you find them, and ask them to share something with you from their past that didn't work so well due to inaccurate thinking. Perhaps it was a purchase, a relationship, or a "good" cause that they sponsored that now, with hindsight, they wish they did not do or make. Given their current viewpoint, what specific advice can they give to you today about thinking ahead with insight and foresight, instead of looking back in hindsight and regret? Record their answers and compare their responses to the advice that Dr. Hill gives.

Chapter 42

Consciously draw to yourself all the Vital Force you need to fill in the mold of right conditions—breathe it in—then see yourself pouring that Vital Force into the conditions or objects you desire.
– Robert Collier

Are you one to believe in coincidences and synchronicities? I do because I have noticed when we engage our psychic abilities things do seem to come together. By utilizing our innate talent through paying attention and practice we often encounter what we expect to find. Carl Jung believed in synchronicity and often wrote on the topic. He looked inward and then by focusing outward and paying close attention he was able to see evidence of things unseen that others may have overlooked.

Let me give you two examples that I noticed recently. Two friends of mine are in Paris now and enjoying the time of their lives. For years, my friend Loretta has been anticipating going, waiting for the opportunity to go, and placing herself mentally in Paris by reflecting on what a trip there would be like. Finally, the day arrived when she and her husband left for France. Flashback—several years ago I had given her a perpetual travel calendar that she has on the front desk of their office. I have one too. As I turned the page to today's date just after they left, what appears exactly on today's date but a glorious photograph of the Eiffel Tower. I took a photo on my phone and sent it to them as a reminder that what we think about we bring about. I believe that their subconscious minds recorded that picture year after year as they flipped the calendar and brought them to just where they were supposed to be this year. Odd? Yes. Impossible? No.

My second example is another simple one. I create daily to-do lists, and as I think of something that needs my attention, I write it down before it escapes my conscious thought. The last item I wrote down this morning showed up just as I arrived at my desk. A craftsman named Joe who created an award for us needed to be reimbursed for his work. I wanted to give him a call and ask him to stop by so that I could pay him. Today, the last item on my to-do list arrived right on schedule the first thing this morning as he walked through the door and literally saved me from making the call. He stated, "I thought that I would just stop in." And, we all know that "thoughts are things" and do materialize when we call them forth. Joe materialized right on schedule and received his payment too! As for me, my item was successfully crossed off my to-do list with no more effort than thinking about it.

When we sharpen the saw of our psychic tool we can begin to build a psychic path that leads us forward into our preferred future. It doesn't just happen. We have to focus on it, be aware, and be receptive, and then as Dr. Hill states: "things begin to show up right on schedule." So quickly too that he tells us that we may wonder where they were hiding all along. Now that we know how to locate the mechanism to fulfill our dreams, why not work to make all our dreams come true?" You can do it if you believe you can.

How to Achieve Creative Vision

by Napoleon Hill

Personal achievement, power, fame and riches: each has a definite price, and the man with *creative vision* not only knows the price but is willing to pay it.

The man with *creative vision* understands the benefits of sharing his blessings, his experiences and his opportunities with others, for he recognizes that only by this method can he attain and enjoy enduring prosperity, happiness and the respect of other men.

The man with *creative vision* also understands that combined creative vision of several minds, directed toward a definite end in a spirit of harmony, is the very heart of the master mind principle and that this type of *creative vision* is a tremendous source of power.

If you feel that there may be a need for *creative vision* as a guiding force in your life, you might begin to develop it by getting on better terms with your own conscience, inspiring yourself with greater self-reliance, providing yourself with a *definite major purpose* in life, and keeping your mind so busy with that purpose that you have no time left for fear and doubt.

You might also adopt the habit of the *silent hour* during which you will be alone with yourself and your Creator. This is one hour you cannot share with any other. You must go into the silence alone, and when you are there, you must speak for yourself. Nothing will happen in your life except that which you inspire by the use of your own initiative.

Nothing of great importance ever happens to anyone without some exercise of *personal initiative*.

Creative vision is the power which inspires the development of *personal initiative*.

PMA Science of Success, Educational Edition. Napoleon Hill Foundation, 1961, p. 420.

Action Assignment #42

Exercise your psychic muscle. Notice daily when things just seem to come together for you in a positive manner. Consider whether or not you have forecast these events prior to their happening. Perhaps you created a mental image, assembled a vision board, vocalized affirmations, repeated positive suggestions, practiced self-hypnosis, or emotionalized what you wanted by creating a burning desire for the picture perfect end result. Whatever it was, if you helped it on its way once, you can do it again and again. Practice makes perfect. Practice noticing and next drawing to you what it is you desire. Reread the Six Steps to Riches in *Think and Grow Rich* and actually complete the steps. Write them out. Then sign the document and date it. This is your actual contract with yourself. Next, stand aside and watch the fireworks, because if you can conceive it, and believe it, you most certainly can achieve it.

Chapter 43

Once when I was living in the heart of a pomegranate, I heard a seed saying, "Someday I shall become a tree, and the wind will sing in my branches, and the sun will dance on my leaves, and I shall be strong and beautiful through all the seasons."

– Kahlil Gibran

Napoleon Hill has stated that life is a chessboard and the player opposite us is time. How true and accurate this is. As we mature, time seems to escalate and the seasons arrive on the heels of each other sometimes spiraling out of control. Before Halloween is here, the stores are dressed in all their holiday glory for Christmas and the festivities of the season. How can we stay focused and grounded, when everything around us is advancing so quickly? Sometimes it seems that we are the ones out of step and the awkward part of the total picture.

We do not have to accept this fact. Daily rituals assist in keeping us grounded in the here and now. Seasonal decorations at home contribute to keeping us in place. Our homes are our castles and we can keep the seasons at bay as long as we want to by closing the front door on early arrivals and remembering to go with the natural flow of nature. By being in the now of Cosmic Habitforce we can relate to where nature wants us to be at this moment in time, and not force anything sooner than we are ready. Each season has its beauty and also its incubation time. If we hurry it up, it is like hurrying up the caterpillar in becoming a butterfly. If forced, the emerging butterfly will wither and die because it has been denied the opportunity to strengthen its wings in the struggle of shedding the cocoon. We too need to strengthen our metaphorical wings before we encounter something new—such as a new season, a new way of seeing, new ideas, and new experiences. In order to ready ourselves for what is to come, we need to be strong and not weak because too much stimulation has assaulted our minds and bodies. Strength comes, but it comes in its appropriate time.

Do not allow outside forces to tell you how to be. Ready yourself for advancement, but only move ahead when you feel the time is right. Pushing forward is good if you are prepared, but can be detrimental if you are not. Each of us blossoms when our time is right. Each of us is unique and may not perform on schedule to the timing of others. Bloom when you are ready. Your timing may be different, but the result will be marvelous all the same.

Personal Relationships

by Napoleon Hill

It is the rarest circumstance to find two people anywhere, at any time, who are related to one another in a spirit of perfect harmony and understanding. Look around you. Take inventory of the relationships of those whom you know best, and you will realize how true this is.

Friction, conflict, and misunderstandings interrupt friendly relationships and cause useless waste of time in almost every walk of life, although common sense should convince anyone that harmony is the only common meeting ground on which men may coordinate their efforts for their mutual benefit.

It is every man's duty to achieve personal success, and every normal person desires to be successful in his chosen occupation. Inasmuch as success is inseparably associated with human relationships, it is an important part of a man's duty to choose his associates with great care.

The successful man may have sympathy for the man who is a failure, but he will not permit it to contaminate his own mind with the defeatist's mental attitude. He will recognize that it would be better for him to suffer loneliness than to associate intimately with those whose minds are contaminated with thoughts of failure and distress.

PMA Science of Success, Educational Edition. Napoleon Hill Foundation, 1961, pp. 465–466.

Action Assignment #43

Create a small altar, shrine or decoration in your home that correlates with the season you are in now.

Next, align with your personal life. Have photos nearby of yourself and others as you enjoy this time of year. For example, if it is fall where you live, consider gathering acorns, colorful leaves, seeds, and photos of friends, family, and others doing things that are done now. Place these items where you can frequently see them and reflect with gratitude for the experiences provided. This serves the purpose of keeping you grounded in the now, and also promotes gratitude for what currently exists in your life.

Chapter 44

After the universal power gives man life … then it is up to man to choose to do with it as he sees fit.

– J. Martin Kohe

One of the purposes of education is to illuminate. Metaphorically this could mean to shed light where there is none. When a person receives instruction and takes it to heart his or her mind can become enlightened with the new information that changes past ways of thinking and doing. It is an inside transformation that shines through on the outside via a person's actions. The center of power is inside and the light emanates from the inside out.

Too often the "razzle dazzle" of performance disrupts a person's true capacity to learn. If the lesson seems to be too easy and smooth, it probably is. Good teachers are not entertainers first, although they may use that strategy in getting the point across. True teachers strengthen their students' capacity to succeed in living their own lives, not in vicariously living someone else's life or lifestyle.

In *Hamlet*, William Shakespeare states:

This above all: to thine ownself be true,
And it must follow, as the night the day,
Thou canst not then be false to any man.

The capacity to grow and change requires that a person is true to their calling first. If we allow someone else to define who we are by accepting their interpretation of how we should live our life, then we forfeit our ability to discover the process and grow ourselves. By allowing others to exploit us, we are giving them control over our greatest power which is the power to choose for ourselves. Surely, there are many paths that can be followed on life's journey. But the truest path is the one that each of us discovers and walks for ourselves.

Simply put, if you are not controlling your own thoughts you are being dominated by someone else's thoughts. Find the truth of your existence within yourself and you will never be exploited because then you will see things as they really are: clearly and distinctly. Become yourself and you will not be swayed by the "razzle dazzle" the world offers. Remember, the sparkle attracts but it holds no real worth.

The Passkey to All Achievement

by Napoleon Hill

Most of us are interested in getting some other member or members of the race to do that which we want them to do. We lie awake nights trying to think out schemes whereby we can get another person to do that which we want him to do. We know exactly how we could make a million dollars, or build a great business, or reduce the cost of living, or render mankind some other great service, *if*— and that eternal if is this:

"If" we could get people to do that which we want them to do!

Seemingly, it has never occurred to most of us that there is an infallible method through which we can get other people to do that which we want them to do. Seemingly, it has never occurred to us that we can get other people to act toward us as we wish them to by simply acting that way toward them first and keeping it up until they respond!

Do you get the full significance of that which you have just read?

If you do, you are to be congratulated, because you will never again complain that anyone failed to do that which you wanted him to do. You will know how to get that which you want by first giving the same thing to some other member or group of members of the human race.

Furthermore, you will never again be guilty of putting into motion a cause which will bring suffering and sorrow and hunger and deprivation to any member of the human race, because you will know beforehand that this same result will eventually come back to curse you.

Napoleon Hill's Golden Rules. The Napoleon Hill Foundation, John Wiley & Sons, 2009, pp. 207–208.

Action Assignment #44

In the *Wizard of Oz*, Dorothy states: "If I ever go looking for my heart's desire again, I won't look any further than my own backyard, because if it isn't there, I never really lost it."

Consider several occasions when you have looked "without" instead of looking "within." Perhaps as you looked for the pot of gold at the end of the rainbow, you actually enabled someone to find theirs by convincing you of their wizardry. These "bad wizards" work only in their behalf, and only have their personalized interests at heart. Remember the times that you fell in a hole in the sidewalk because you weren't looking where you were going.

In order to avoid the pitfalls in life, you must first listen to your own heart and then journey down that path. Just as Dorothy does, you have always had the ability to go home. Your internal compass knows the way and every time you journey within you will arrive safe and sound in the outside world.

Chapter 45

Since the beginning of time, there have been people purporting to have the secret to success. Success is a self-fulfilling prophecy, and there are as many definitions of success as there are people in the world.

– Jim Stovall

Each of us is born unique. There are no duplicates—even twins grow and develop differently in many diverse ways. Likewise, what makes us happy, contributes to our success, and enriches our life is not random but specific to whom we are as well. It is as if we are a musical instrument in life's symphony and our specialized gifts and talents contribute to the composition as a whole. The instrument we play is who we are, but the ultimate song is a unified team effort.

Until we define our definite major purpose in life and call it into focus, we are like a boat afloat on the ocean without means of journeying anywhere. E. M. Forster asks: *"How do I know what I think until I see what I say?"* Personal maturity demands that we act out our life's mission. Thinking about it is never enough. We must apply it in community so that we can share our special gifts and talents with the world. That is why we are here!

Don't allow someone else to define who you are. No matter if it is a family member, friend, or employer, only you can determine your ultimate path in life. When we acquiesce and allow someone to tell us how we are to behave, what we are to think, what we should purchase, and where we should live and work, we are giving away our greatest gift. By defining who we are and why we are here, we create our life's work. No one else is equipped to do it exactly the way we can.

So, advance in your own path. Achieve your mission by first defining your purpose and then acting upon it. Application is the key to learning and progress. You must do something with what you know in order to advance to the next level. Asking someone to do it for you, or not doing it yourself is not permissible. You must walk the path for yourself. Then when you truly arrive at your success, you will feel a great sense of reward and accomplishment because the achievement belongs solely to you and not to someone else.

Success Consciousness

by Napoleon Hill

You have it within your power to acquire a success consciousness which will prove the perfect antidote for fear. Definiteness of purpose is the beginning of such a success consciousness. Find out what it is you want from life and look for it all the time. Demand much! Set a high goal, and believe that you will, with the aid of Infinite Intelligence, reach that goal. Then get into action! Here is a poem which expresses this truth very well:

I bargained with Life for a penny
And Life would pay no more;
However, I begged at evening
When I counted my scanty store.

For Life is a just employer;
He gives you whatever you ask.
But once you have set the wages,
Why, you must bear the task.

I worked for a menial's hire
Only to learn dismayed
That any wage I had asked of Life,
Life would have willingly paid.

–Jessie B. Rittenhouse

Successful men do not bargain with life for poverty! They know that there is a power through which life may be made to pay off on their own terms. They know that this power is available to every man who comes into possession of his own mind. Carve out a career! Don't bore your way through life.

> The man who acquires the ability to take full possession of his own mind may take possession of everything else to which he is justly entitled....
>
> –*Andrew Carnegie*

PMA Science of Success, Educational Edition. Napoleon Hill Foundation, 1961, p. 95.

Action Assignment #45

Construct a wheel with 12 spokes on a sheet of paper. On each spoke write one of the twelve riches of life that Dr. Hill identifies. They are: a positive mental attitude, sound physical health, harmony in human relationships, freedom from fear, the hope of achievement, the capacity for faith, the willingness to share one's blessings, a labor of love, an open mind on all subjects, self-discipline, the capacity to understand people, and financial security.

Starting at the center with point zero and progressing outward to a ten, pinpoint your progression on each of these twelve characteristics of a life richly lived. For example, you may be a 5 on the capacity for faith, a 7 on sound physical health, but only a three on self-discipline. When completed, connect the dots. Notice the shape of your wheel that now represents your alignment with life's riches. Decide how you can balance out your wheel by focusing on and improving the traits that need work. Balance here is the key to stability and satisfaction. As you rate yourself, you will see just what you need to work on next in order to have a full and balanced life.

Chapter 46

The Gospel of Wealth but echoes Christ's words; it calls upon the millionaire to sell all he hath and give the highest and best to the poor, by administering his estate for his fellow men before he is called to lie down and rest upon the bosom of mother earth.
– Andrew Carnegie

As we journey through life it is good to consider what contribution we have made to humanity as a whole. If we have left the world improved and not diminished by our presence, then we have made a deposit and not a withdrawal. By consciously thinking about the good we can do now—today—we do not postpone our gift while living. Initially, we train our interior self to see where we have been the recipients of good, and then in turn we go the extra mile by giving back. Being grateful for daily gifts lifts up our thoughts to a higher realm because where there are gifts there is a Giver. By acknowledging this generosity that comes from afar, we condition ourselves to become like-minded in both thought and deed.

By taking small steps that serve as a prelude to giving, we increase our awareness as to the wonder and benevolence in the world. We see the morning sky, smell the autumn leaves, feel the silky fur of our pet, taste the diverse foods we eat, hear the seasonal sounds of the outdoors, and sense that this is all placed here for our enjoyment. What remarkable things for us to receive upon entering this world via the gift of the senses.

Begin today to be a giver. A kind word, recognition, praise, and a listening ear are all things that can be given that are free of cost. Spend time with a person who has suffered a loss, read to a child who needs attention, brown bag a lunch for two and share with a friend, invite someone over for coffee and homemade cake, walk with someone who wants to exercise, offer a ride to someone unable to drive, and brainstorm with others regarding things you can do to contribute to making someone's life a little better. Keep a list and do several things each week, or at least one GEM (Going the Extra Mile) action per day.

You will be compensated with lightness of spirit, enthusiasm for living, spontaneous ideas for going beyond where you find yourself today, and an enhanced positive mental attitude. All of these things in exchange for the gifts that you give to someone else are priceless and not for sale. You first have to earn them by giving of yourself, and in exchange you will receive far more than you have given to begin with every time. Try it for a week and see. You will truly be amazed at your capacity to give, right here, right now, in this moment! Do it for someone else, and do it for you too!

The Gifts from Giving

by Napoleon Hill

Form the habit of tolerance and keep an open mind on all subjects, toward people of all races and creeds. Learn to like people just as they are, instead of demanding of them that they be as you wish them to be.

Recognize that love and affection constitute the finest medicines for both your body and your soul. Love changes the entire chemistry of the body and conditions it for the expression of a *positive mental attitude*. And love also extends the space you may occupy in the hearts of your fellowmen. And in this connection it is important to remember that while love is free, the best way to receive it is to give it.

Keep a daily diary of your good deeds in behalf of others, and never let the sun set on a single day without recording some act of human kindness. The benefits of this habit will be cumulative and eventually it will give you domain over great spaces in the hearts of your fellowmen. And remember: *One good deed each day will keep old man gloom away.*

For every favor or benefit you receive give an equal benefit to others. The law of increasing returns will operate in your favor and eventually ... perhaps very soon ... it will give you the capacity to get everything you are entitled to receive. A *positive mental attitude* must have a two-way highway on which to travel, or it will cease to function.

PMA Science of Success, Educational Edition. Napoleon Hill Foundation, 1961, p. 228–229.

Action Assignment #46

Start with the alphabet and create a giving tree. Each of the 26 leaves on this tree will represent 26 things that you have actually given this month.

For example, using letters A, B, and C you might write on your first three leaves, "Able-bodied and willing to assist someone who isn't, I raked my neighbor's leaves." "Because I could afford to, I donated grocery items to a local food bank." And, "Caring what happens to outdoor birds during the winter, I keep my yard feeder stocked with seed." Now, following these hints, create your own giving tree. You will feel an enormous sense of satisfaction from not just imagining what you will do, but by actually doing the things you contemplate. Giving takes practice, so the assignment this week requires you to practice what you preach.

Chapter 47

Starting with something which the child knows through experience, and is therefore personally interested in, the subject is thenceforth to be progressively developed.

– Patterson DuBois

As a teacher for many years, I know for certain that the closer you align the lesson to meet your student where he or she is in the present, the greater the opportunity for instructional success. Although many well-meaning people seek to challenge students by aiming at something far beyond their reach, the teacher with insight challenges their students to take incremental steps toward their desired outcomes. Too often by focusing on potential possibilities in the far distant future, dreams become wishes rather than goals. Napoleon Hill states: "If wishes were horses, beggars would ride." By this, he means that wishes produce no predictable outcome other than more wishes. Beggars do not mount stately steeds based on wishes. Knights mount impressive steeds based upon their performance.

Aligning the lesson with both a point of contact for the student and finding that teachable moment almost guarantees that the lesson will be well-received and integrated. Biblically, thinking about the parables that Christ used as his instructional material aligns with this type of lesson planning. By narrating simple stories that people could relate to because of the nature of humankind, Christ impacted his audience through storytelling at its finest. He knew the culture of his audience, and he sought to blend his teaching with his simply profound messages for greatest impact. The result is that these parables have and still do change people's lives for the better.

If you wish to enable a student to progressively become a better version of him or herself, first attempt to learn the culture and the daily environment that they inhabit. By knowing where they currently reside, you can bring up the next opportunity that they can realistically strive for as they develop. Christ did not tell people to strive for sainthood, rather he instructed them in the process of living a better life. And, if that eventually led to sainthood, it just underscored the sequential process to be followed.

Aim to be a practitioner who recognizes the moment in time that a student can be engaged, and then know the point of contact that can capture that student's interest and attention. When you discern these two opportunities, your lesson will be received and integrated. And, it is worth all the background work that you have to do in order to make this happen because then you will have opened that window of opportunity just enough to allow a glimpse of the improved life not in the far distant future but just around the corner.

Adults—Little Children Grown Tall

by Napoleon Hill

In a sense, adults are only little children grown tall, and we do best that which we have been influenced to wish to do. We also resent being forced to do anything. This is an inherent trait of all mankind, and it prevails at all ages, under all circumstances. Everyone likes the freedom with which he may move on his own initiative. Destroy this freedom and you retard the mental and spiritual growth of the individual. You might also say that you retard economic and financial achievements the moment you destroy the desire for personal freedom based on the privilege of *personal initiative*. Organized thought leads to spiritual and mental growth provided it is expressed through action. One does not grow spiritually or mentally by thought alone. *Growth is the result of thought expressed through voluntary and definitely controlled habits of action.*

Ability, in its most effective form, is the result of thought expressed through organized action. Theory forms a helpful background for ability, but it is not enough to insure success. That is why the college graduate must acquire practical experience before he becomes a man of ability. Theoretical learning is an essential foundation of education, but it is only a foundation. *An educated person is one who has developed his mind through a combination of theory and practice so that he can shape any set of circumstances to meet the requirements of his desires and deeds.*

PMA Science of Success, Educational Edition. Napoleon Hill Foundation, 1961, p. 322–323.

Action Assignment #47

Points of Contact or Teachable Moments often enter into our lives unawares and surprisingly leave lasting, lifelong impressions that remain with us until we make our exit from the planet.

Consider your timeline in life so far—birth to where you are now—and recall five touchstone moments in time that created a new awareness, expansion of thinking, greater insight, and possibly a new focus or direction in life. Perhaps these lessons were delivered by a teacher, a parent, a relative, a minister, or friend who was there to conduct the instruction. Or, possibly, an event in your life presented the lesson. However it occurred, the lesson learned at the crucial moment in time is what we are after for your timeline. Perhaps, figuratively or realistically, you were at a fork in the road and this lesson, with just the right point of contact, played into your teachable moment.

First reflect and next position these five transitional moments on your timeline. Consider what it would have meant if you had not received this information in a timely fashion. Where would you be now and what would you be doing? By recalling and considering these moments in time, we can gain insight as to how we shaped our lives to date and how we can continue to shape them in the future.

CHAPTER 48

Man did not weave the web of life; he is merely a Strand in it.
Whatever he does to the web, He does to himself.
– Chief Seattle of the Dwamish Tribe

Rituals create memories. During this season of Thanksgiving, think back to earlier times when you celebrated the holidays by following established rituals. Whether it was a sit down dinner with all the trimmings, a game of scrabble, a morning or evening walk, playing Christmas albums, watching the parade on television as the meal is cooking, or just looking at the sales that herald the shopping season—all of these are repeated performances that turn into rituals when done over and over again. These actions help to create continuity with the transition of the seasons.

For me personally, the season of fall brings both endings and beginnings. As we prepare the yard for winter, the garden and flowers are gone, but the earth takes a much needed recuperative rest as it prepares for the next season. Beddings for animals are created as they need a warm and safe place to pass the winter months. Lights are turned on earlier, as the days grow shorter, and eventually the landscape changes from the vibrant greens, oranges, and yellows of late Indian Summer to the expansive whiteness of the first snow. People slow down, and rest more as the change of seasons brings about a sense of hibernation for us too.

This time of transition can be used for family gatherings, more indoor activities, and less focus on the external. It is a time for going within to eventually produce more without. Activity has not ceased, but only changed, resting, in order to accumulate the strength for the spring production that is just around the corner. The poet Shelley wisely asks: "If winter comes, can spring be far behind?"

So, look at this season of rituals as a time to step back and enjoy the downtime that Cosmic Habitforce has gifted to us. It is a time for planning, for internal renewal, for growth that cannot be seen but is uniquely present in the creative seed within our souls. Use this time to consider where you are now, and where you would like to be. Just be. Enjoy the moment. Cherish the time given to you. And, wisely prepare for the new stage of growth that is just around the corner.

Creed of Thanksgiving for Riches

by Napoleon Hill

Money is the most common form of wealth and hence financial security is the most sought-after goal. Our entire national economy is based on the profit motive and let us hope that nothing ever happens to remove or stifle that incentive of reward for personal initiative. It is the basis of the American way of life.

Is it any wonder then, that the desire for wealth or gain is a powerful motive for action? Uncontrolled, this desire leads to greed. When it is controlled and guided by a worthwhile definite goal, it is a source of constructive action which may bless and enrich the lives of men and women.

Our suggested creed concerning material riches may be summarized in a few short statements:

> I give thanks daily, not for mere riches, but for wisdom with which to recognize, embrace, and properly use the great abundance of riches I now have at my command. I have no enemies because I injure no man for any cause, but I try to benefit all with whom I come in contact, by teaching the way to enduring riches. I have more material wealth

than I need because I am free from greed and covet only the material things I can use while I live.

PMA Science of Success, Educational Edition. Napoleon Hill Foundation, 1961, p. 25.

Action Assignment #48

This is the season for making lists. Lists help keep us organized. They are the mundane and daily activities that we write down unless we forget to pay the taxes, pick up the dry cleaning, keep the dentist's appointment, and get our flu shot. Lists keep us focused and prepared for advancement in our lives. When we write it down we begin the process of dedicating our time to making it happen. Lists become contracts with ourselves to do something—anything—that earns a spot on our daily itinerary. In a similar way, they can predispose us to success. When we establish a goal, write it down, and take subsequent action steps towards its completion, we are holding ourselves accountable for what it is that we want to do.

Consider making several lists this week. One can be a daily list of items that must be done in order to keep your life functioning on schedule. Another can be a list that positions you on your path to success as you define it. What action steps do you need to take in order to arrive on schedule? Are you buying a new car, new home, retiring within five years, or planning a special trip? Prepare now. Set those goals, look at the calendar, and then weekly, if not daily, put pen to paper and chart your course. Planners succeed but those who only dream never establish the foundations for their dreams unless they put their dreams into a workable plan, and then work that plan. Be a doer and all your dreams can and will be fulfilled.

Chapter 49

We don't need to look for heroes, because they are among us every day. All we have to do is pay attention and stay alert, and you will see amazing things being done on a regular basis by regular people, who never look for recognition or praise.

– Dan Kudulis

Lessons learned from living are the most valuable ones. These experiential happenings often "cut us to the quick" as the Wizard of Oz tells Dorothy when she challenges his authenticity. Doing intensifies and cements the experience because it is in the "doing" that we live, move, and have our being. Through our bodies we internalize the experience and that is what makes it more profound.

Unless you have directly experienced something, you may think you understand what the actual feeling is like, but it is not until you do that you will know the difference between an imagined occurrence and an actual experience. The difference is intense. Many times people console others by saying "I know how you feel," but those who actually have walked in your footsteps comfort with just silence and their physical presence. Words do not suffice.

In this lifetime, we are spiritual beings having a physical experience. This experience is tied to the lessons that we are here to learn. All lessons are not popular or positive ones. Many are horrific and feel like a sucker punch right in the solar plexus. Once experienced, it is hard to forget something like that, so we learn a valuable lesson and keep on living but with eyes now wide open.

Death forces us into accountability with life. We already know the end result, but why is it we defer the good that we can now do until the opportunity has passed us by? Regret does not feel as good as joy in a job well done. When we are enthusiastic, passionate, and living the life we imagine, in the time of loss we will have stored up good memories that serve to console us. It is comforting to know that we contributed to the good of the whole, and did not fail to act when the opportunity was there for us.

Today, just for once do something extraordinary for someone who least expects it and maybe doesn't "deserve" it. Feel the good that you can create and do it just to delight in the experience of playing the role of "do-gooder." Each and every one of us can be a philanthropist if we just act on our highest imaginings. What legacy of experiences are you actualizing now?

A Christmas Card from Mother

by W. Clement Stone

My mother.... As the sun was about to rise one summer's morning, her spirit departed from a full and happy life. She was ready.

Fall followed summer, then winter—Christmas morning arrived.

On the breakfast table this eventful Christmas morning was a beautiful Christmas card from ... Mother. The writing on the envelope was unmistakably hers ... just the name: Clement.

Perhaps because of the suddenness of this pleasant surprise—perhaps because of the habit of seeing my name on the envelope containing a Christmas card from Mother each Christmas morning—perhaps because I believe in miracles—or perhaps in the thrill and expectancy of reaching for the envelope to open it, I did not at first think this strange.

As I read and enjoyed the pleasurable surprise of seeing her very discernible handwriting in the signature—"Mother"—a feeling of amazement came over me. A Christmas card from Mother!

After a long pause, I read the card to those she loved so dearly: Jessie, Clem, Donna and Norman ... my wife and my children.

As I was reading, I kept seeking a logical explanation for—A Christmas Card from Mother. (If you would like the explanation, if you would like to learn how to make someone truly happy on Christmas Day or a birthday, read below.)

Explanation of a Christmas Card from Mother

While getting out our Christmas ornaments, Mrs. Stone ran across many of the lovely Christmas cards we had saved, including ... A Christmas Card from Mother. My wife's thoughtfulness in placing the card at my breakfast place brought me much happiness. Perhaps you can give this joy to a dear one, too.

Success Unlimited. W. Clement Stone, December, 1962, pp. 2 & 17.

Action Assignment #49

It's time for your letter to Santa.

Do you have an idea or problem that you or the world needs to work on today? Write a letter detailing your heartfelt concern to Santa—either personal or global—and request the gift of a solution from this humble St. Nicholas. As you state the problem, be aware of potential ideas and perhaps solutions that come to mind. Whether fantasy or reality, write them down as they occur. As you brainstorm within your letter, consider how by composing your letter you are setting up the expectation for an answer. Give yourself freedom to be a seeker of a positive outcome even if your reality is currently negative. Write your "Dear Santa" letter on your best stationery, in your best hand-writing, and place it in an envelope. Remember to date and sign it too.

Now, put it right where you know Santa will find it, and listen in your heart to hear his response. When the time is right, once again put pen to paper and allow Santa to dictate his response to you. Expect a miracle. Santa always delivers on schedule!

Chapter 50

Love is never a sign of weakness, but rather of great strength. And in order to be fully appreciated and enjoyed, love must be shared. We must never try to keep our love secret.

– Andrew Bienkowski & Mary Akers

Do you ever wonder what part is more valuable—the gift, the giver, or the "giftee?" Whenever a person strives to find just the right gift for the right person at the right time it often becomes a process of anticipating just what the other person needs or wants from the giver's perspective. Too often the giver's taste and style enters into the equation and the recipient is given what the giver would like to receive. That accounts for many "repurposed" gifts.

Sometimes the recipient requests what they would like, and the process is simplified but then a great deal of the fun of shopping for and finding just the perfect gift is removed since that has already been decided. The giver's ideas, attitudes, styles, and tastes do not count. The gift becomes a practical one, and although useful it seldom becomes one of those treasured for a lifetime.

And then there is the gift. This is the perfect gift that waits patiently for the customer to encounter it at just the right moment for just the right person at just the right time. This is comparable to an art form that few people ever accomplish in the art of giving. But when it happens, the sky opens and the light on the recipient's face makes the search worthwhile. It is something to strive for even if it is rarely achieved. And, you will know when and if you hit the bull's-eye on this one by the receiver's response.

What it comes down to is that giving is a reciprocal process that doesn't start with a giver and end with the receiver. In order to be fulfilling the process must come back around and operate like a series of non-ending circles. People should give to give and not give to get. Whenever the "getting" overrules the "giving" selfishness and greed grow. It is in the giving of ourselves in the process that allows the giver to grow and become a greater and more sensitive person, and likewise it is the desire in the recipient to return the favor that makes it a cyclic, replicating process.

The mandate should be to include yourself in your giving. Don't make the gift generic; make it as special as you are in order for the recipient to remember the gift and your thoughtfulness for days and even years to come.

Good Habits

by Napoleon Hill

Form the habit of saying or doing something every day which will make another person, or persons feel better. You can do this by a phone call, a kind word in passing, dropping a postal card, or by doing some other kindness for another. A good inspirational book placed in the hand of one who needs it could, for example, work wonders in the life of that person.

Recognize that the space you occupy in this world is in exact ratio to the quality and the quantity of the service you render for the benefit of others, plus the mental attitude in which you render it.

PMA Science of Success, Educational Edition. Napoleon Hill Foundation, 1961, pp. 225–226.

Action Assignment #50

Consider one person on your Christmas list. Spend a few moments recording what their likes are and consider how you might match their tastes of a special unique and thoughtful gift. Embark on a shopping spree at your local church craft sale, the community resale shops, the sale bins at the library, and seek out that perfect gift for someone that is not costly, but considerate of who they are. Perhaps set a small limit to what you will spend, but be extravagant in the thought and caring that you put into the selection. Maybe this gift is for a secret friend, a random name draw at an office party, or for someone you just care about.

When your selection is made, write an accompanying note to the person saying why you selected what you did and how it relates to who they are. Even if you miss the target, you will be remembered for your caring and consideration in trying to give a gift that matches their interests.

Chapter 51

Surprisingly, I receive a lot of letters from adults, and not surprisingly, their letters and their hearts are filled with sadness, disappointment, pessimism, negativity, doubt and even anger—quite a laundry list that they should deal with themselves. There's only so much a toymaker can do.

– Santa Claus

This Holiday, no matter your faith, do unto others. In this manner, you too will enjoy your good works. Our joy can be doubled just by extending ourselves to friends and strangers. Using the prayer of St. Francis, let's pause between the lines in order to offer a few suggestions of what doing something for another might look like.

A Prayer by St. Francis of Assisi

Lord,

Make me an instrument of Your peace.
Nip an argument or disagreement in the bud by deciding not to respond negatively.
Where there is hatred let me sow love;
Speak words of kindness and praise in the midst of a volatile situation. Ask respectfully if you might say a prayer.
Where there is injury, pardon;
Hold no one but yourself accountable for a minor injury. Don't kick the dog or cat who causes you to stumble or fall.

Where there is doubt, faith;
Offer sympathy with the certainty of faith. In sadness faith, hope, and charity are healers.
Where there is despair, hope;
Ask how you can best help in this time of trouble.
Where there is darkness, light;
Sweep a littered floor, cook a meal, wash a dirty dish, replace a light bulb, put items away, and create orderliness.
and
Where there is sadness, joy.
Tell a story from a previous time with a happy ending.

Grant that I may not so much
Seek to be consoled as to console;
Hold a spontaneous service for someone who has experienced a loss—of a family member, friend, relative, or pet.
To be understood as to understand;
Allow someone to share a different point of view, and this time really listen.
To be loved as to love;
Tell friends and family members you love them before your hang up the phone every time you talk.
For it is in giving that we receive;
Double all your pleasure by sharing what you have with another person rather than saving or storing it.
It is in pardoning that we are pardoned;
Forgive and forget past injuries now and forever.
and
It is in dying that we are born to eternal life.
Accept the plan the Creator has for each and every one of us and fear not because others have gone before us and we need to have faith in what has been promised.

Courtesy

by Napoleon Hill

Someone has said that courtesy is the cheapest, yet the most profitable, of all traits of a pleasing personality. This may be an exaggeration, but it is not an overstatement to say that courtesy is an essential trait of personality without which no one may become pleasing to his associates.

As to its price, we must admit that it is absolutely free. All it costs is: a positive mental attitude, sincerity of purpose, consideration for the rights and feelings of others, and a willingness to share your blessings with your fellowmen. Observe how all of these principles are interrelated so that the development of one leads to the achievement of others.

Courtesy is the habit of respecting other people's rights and feelings under all circumstances; the habit of going out of your way to help a less fortunate person whenever possible; the habit of rendering useful service without the expectation of direct reward; and last, but not least, the habit of controlling selfishness, greed, envy and hatred.

Courtesy is a reflection of the spirit of fellowship without which no one may have dependable friends. It will often serve as an irresistible force with which one may disarm enemies and antagonists.

PMA Science of Success, Educational Edition. Napoleon Hill Foundation, 1961, pp. 225–226.

Action Assignment #51

While out and about enjoying the hustle and bustle of the season, practice offering random acts of kindness that are directed towards both friends and strangers. Here are some simple ideas:

Compliment someone on their appearance. Greet someone as they walk by you. Smile.

Be a Secret Santa and leave a small gift for someone to find. Select a "wish" tied on a holiday tree and fulfill it. Pick up the tab for someone's morning coffee and roll. Lose a dollar on purpose for someone to find. Recall the song, "That's What I Like About You," and compose a list of your own for a special person who needs a pick-me-up. Rewrite a favorite holiday song and customize the lyrics for someone needing to catch the spirit of the season. Send an unsigned bouquet. Leave a small token in someone's mailbox or hanging on their front door. Tip double. And, scatter birdseed for our feathered friends. Now, it's your turn. Create a daily calendar of giving that promotes the good news because you changed the world one humble considerate act at a time.

CHAPTER 52

Health is not our decision. Sure, we can exercise, eat right, take some vitamins and the medicines that the doctor prescribes, but health is ultimately in God's hands. Happiness, by contrast, is a choice. It's an attitude, a decision and a way of life.

– Rich Winograd

This week marks the close to the year filled with Action Assignments. If you have completed each one you may notice that you are more energetic and open to taking control of the outcomes in your life. Even small steps that are action oriented enable a person to feel in control of what is occurring in their daily lives. It is important to eliminate the inertia that can occur when a person is comfortable remaining at rest. Rest is good but only for the period it is required. A person is built for action, and unless action prevails the consequence of doing nothing is a downward spiral.

Now it is your turn to create the actions that you will take in your life. When I am overwhelmed or simply lazy, I ask the simple question, "What should I do next?" An answer always comes and it always contributes to the good of the whole. Procrastination reinforces the downward cycle because the promise of doing it later when conditions are perfect is the quintessential lure for doing nothing. If you are troubled by procrastination, ask yourself the question "What should I do next?" and then do it. Just by doing you show yourself that you can overcome procrastination.

Next, do not do only for yourself but do for others. When we focus on ourselves we become self-centered and judgmental. Do something for someone else and you will reap the rewards of expanding both your awareness and circle of influence. Be sincerely people minded.

Finally, focus on completion and not perfection. Doing the best job you are capable of doing is essential, but being perfect is not. Perfection is not achieved in every single action taken daily. If that were so, most of us would never manage getting out of bed in the morning. You can strive for perfection, but do not let it become a handicap that is an excuse for non-performance.

So by becoming conditioned for ongoing action that takes into consideration both ourselves and others, we are gaining and not losing in the area of personal growth. And, by not insisting on perfection but rather on performance we gain because we grow toward becoming more adept as we perform. We learn by doing, and in the doing we can continue to strive for heightened performance. Therein we find that we grow closer to perfection in whatever it is we are striving for in the doing and not in the delaying! Challenge yourself to success, one small step at a time and eradicate the negatives of inertia, procrastination, the desire for perfection, and the need for selfishness. You can and will become a new and improved version of yourself if you carry on with these simple practices in actions you decree by design.

The Mechanics of How to Proceed

by Napoleon Hill

You know that you will probably never feel that you are completely ready to start any project. There will always be something else you could do in preparation for your take-off. But if you start where you stand and work with whatever tools you have at hand, other and better goals will reveal themselves as you move forward.

Write out a clear, concise statement of your goal, just as though you were writing a letter to a friend, explaining what it is you really desire from life. List the benefits which will result either during the process or after attainment of your major goal.

For example:

1. List the information or knowledge you desire to acquire.
2. List the kind of work you desire to do.
3. List the kind of personality you desire to be.
4. Write down how much you desire to earn and receive each year.
5. List the places you desire to visit and see.
6. List the skills, arts, crafts, and sciences you desire to master.

As you list these, write out a separate statement of the motive which prompts each desire. Each one of us, as a normal human being, does everything he does in response to some one or more of the ten basic motives. Relate each one of the elements in your objective to some strong motive. This will enable you to develop a burning desire behind it and continually impress your subconscious mind until it has a complete preoccupation with the attainment of your aims and purposes.

PMA Science of Success, Educational Edition. Napoleon Hill Foundation, 1961, pp. 41–42.

Action Assignment #52

Consider the actions that you have taken this year and note in a written fashion the results. What did you do, and what were the outcomes—either good or bad? Next, consider the actions that you contemplated taking and likewise note the results that you received—either good or bad. What conclusions can you draw from this review? How can you improve your results for next year? Begin by listing five areas of your life wherein you would like to see improvement. Next, create three actions underneath each area that you can do today! And then do them!

Be your very best always!

"WHATEVER THE MIND CAN CONCEIVE AND BELIEVE, THE MIND CAN ACHIEVE."

For more information about Napoleon Hill and available products, please contact the following locations:

Napoleon Hill World Learning Center
Purdue University Calumet
2300 West 173rd Street
Hammond, Indiana 46323-2094

Judith Williamson, Director
Uriel "Chino" Martinez, Assistant & Graphic Designer
Guang "Alan" Chen, Computer Resource Specialist

Telephone: 219.989.3173 or 219.989.3166
Email: nhf@purduecal.edu

The Napoleon Hill Foundation
University of Virginia – Wise
College Relations Apt. C
1 College Avenue
Wise, Virginia 24293

Don Green, Executive Director
Annedia Sturgill, Executive Assistant

Telephone: 276.328.6700
Email: napoleonhill@uvawise.edu

Website: www.naphill.org